REVIEWS AND ENDORSEMENTS

God's prophetic plan for humanity is true and certain. This work demonstrates the relevance and centrality of the Bible in all of life and the need for every Christian to accurately study and interpret it. I encourage you to read this side-by-side with your Bible.

Timothy J. Demy, Th.D., Ph.D.
Co-author of Answers to Common Questions about the End Times, *by Timothy J. Demy and Thomas Ice*

I endorse and highly recommend Dr. Fred Thompson, both as a person and as a Bible theologian, in the area of converging of Bible Prophecy and world events. He has avoided a slanted United States perspective to grasp the involvement of major nations including third world countries.

His research comes from valid and reliable world sources that document the blending of the world economy, morality, ethics, politics, religion, science and technology which fulfills prophecy of the Last Days.

Once I started reading *Spiritual Tsunami*, I couldn't stop reading until I completed it. It reinforced my faith that God is in control of the future.

Duane E Buhler
Pastor Emeritus, Consultant Christian Faith Center, Nampa, Idaho

I have known Dr. Fred Thompson for the past two years. He and his wife Sandy have been a blessing to me personally and to the hundreds of people who call Christian Faith Center home. He is the type of person who inspires confidence in those around him. Perhaps I can sum up my thoughts toward Dr. Fred with this common adage, "I hope to be like him when I grow up." To say that he is outgoing is an understatement. He is an avid outdoorsman, dearly loves Jesus and His Word, and is a tremendous Bible teacher. You will be blessed and inspired by *Spiritual Tsunami.*

Monty Sears
Senior Pastor, Christian Faith Center, Nampa, Idaho

I am pleased to endorse *Spiritual Tsunami.* Given the world's current environment, every person who has an interest in the future would do well to arm themselves with the best sources to prepare for what may come. Dr. Thompson offers the reader a serious look at the days in which we live and provides a relevant and very plausible Biblical context for understanding modern events. The information provided within the pages of this book will provide a path to higher ground for those who wish to avoid the very real tidal waves that are approaching. The material in this book is practical, easy to follow, and up-to-date. With each page turned the reader is motivated to prayer and to action. This book would also serve as a great study for any one person or group that seeks a better understanding of modern events in light of Biblical truth and end-time prophecy.

Konrad Ziesing
Executive Pastor, Christian Faith Center, Nampa, Idaho
Adjunct Faculty Member, Northwest University

Spiritual Tsunami

Biblical prophecy and world events are converging

DR. FRED THOMPSON

WestBow Press
A Division of Thomas Nelson

Author photo by Dale Crockett. Used by permission.
Rapture/2nd Coming table by Timothy Demy and Thomas Ice in Chapter 20. Used by author permission.

WestBow Press books may be ordered through booksellers or by contacting:

WestBow Press
A Division of Thomas Nelson
1663 Liberty Drive
Bloomington, IN 47403
www.westbowpress.com
1-(866) 928-1240

ISBN: 978-1-4497-3915-7 (sc)
ISBN: 978-1-4497-3916-4 (hc)
ISBN: 978-1-4497-3914-0 (e)

Library of Congress Control Number: 2012901766

Printed in the United States of America

WestBow Press rev. date: 03/09/2012

CONTENTS

Preface vii
Acknowledgments ix
Introduction xi

Chapter 1: Proof-of-Concept Events 1

PART 1: World Economy 5

Chapter 2: Economic Chaos 7
Chapter 3: Oil Discoveries In Israel 27
Chapter 4: City of Babylon 31

PART 2: Morality & Ethics 37

Chapter 5: Moral Decline 39
Chapter 6: Ethical Decline 59

PART 3: Politics 79

Chapter 7: Attacks against Israel 81
Chapter 8: Peace in the Middle East 95
Chapter 9: One World Government 103

PART 4: Religion 125

Chapter 10: Apostasy 127
Chapter 11: Persecution of Believers 131
Chapter 12: Seven Churches Of Asia 135

PART 5: Science & Technology 141

Chapter 13: Environmental Disasters 143
Chapter 14: Science & Technology 161

PART 6: Last Days 173

Chapter 15: The Great "Snatching Away" 175
Chapter 16: Coalition of Countries 187
Chapter 17: Vulture Population 193

Chapter 18: Third Temple in Jerusalem 197
Chapter 19: False Messiahs 201
Chapter 20: Seven Years of Tribulation 205
Chapter 21: Second Coming of Christ 219
Chapter 22: Armageddon 225
Chapter 23: Thousand Year Period 229

Final Thoughts 233

Chapter 24: Final Thoughts 235

Appendices 241

Appendix A Rapture Timelines 243
Appendix B End Times Timeline With Rapture Views 245

Notes 247

List of Abbreviations 271

About the Author 275

PREFACE

Given the condition of the world today, with its economic woes, political crises and conflicts, and events hard to explain by science alone, it is appropriate to add to the volume of words already written concerning the approach of the end times. As a Christian, while reading scripture, the signs of the approach of the times termed *End Times* are looming larger with each passing year.

One does not have to be a Bible scholar to discern the convergence of Biblical prophecy and world events.

In this book we will examine the events reported in the news media alongside scriptures warning of them. Today, one simply has to have the Bible open alongside the newspaper to see the links.

Charles Dickens classic statement in his 1859 novel, *A Tale of Two Cities,* describes the current world situation well:

> "It was the best of times, it was the worst of times, it was the age of wisdom, it was the age of foolishness, it was the epoch of belief, it was the epoch of incredulity, it was the season of Light, it was the season of Darkness, it was the spring of hope, it was the winter of despair, we had everything before us, we had nothing before us, we were all going direct to heaven, we were all going direct the other way—in short, the period was so far like the present period, that some of its noisiest authorities insisted on its being received, for good or for evil, in the superlative degree of comparison only." [1]

ACKNOWLEDGMENTS

My deepest gratitude goes to my Lord and Savior, Jesus Christ, for His inspiration, support and guidance as I undertook the formidable task of chronicling world events and linking them to Biblical prophecy. Three years ago, while teaching classes on the end-times, the Holy Spirit nudged me and quietly suggested that more Christians needed to become aware of the fact that we are seeing events around the world that, in the aggregate, are like the happenings of the end-times and which led to the writing of *Spiritual Tsunami*. Biblical prophecy and world events ***are*** converging!

The support and encouragement of my wife, Sandy, to engage with this subject provided the courage to take on the often-daunting and time-consuming task of researching and writing. Pastor Monty Sears, of Christian Faith Center, Nampa, Idaho, kept me current by allowing me to teach adult Christian Education classes on the subject. Thanks to Dr. William MacLean for a journeyman's job of helping an engineer engage once again with the English language and grammar through his editing and gentle admonishment to better writing.

Thanks also to Robert Lee, who co-taught classes with me on end-times prophecy. And my gratitude goes out to the many friends who challenged me to read, study, and think about the plethora of books and articles on the subject by authors, Bible scholars and theologians who have traveled before me on the pathway of Bible prophecy.

Dr. Fred Thompson

INTRODUCTION

Hard Times, They Are A' Comin'

> *[1] Blessed is the man who does not walk in the counsel of the wicked or stand in the way of sinners or sit in the seat of mockers. . . [4] Not so the wicked! They are like chaff that the wind blows away. [5] Therefore the wicked will not stand in the judgment, nor sinners in the assembly of the righteous. [6] For the LORD watches over the way of the righteous, but the way of the wicked will perish.*
>
> (Ps. 1:1, 4-6 NIV)

There is a spiritual tsunami of events and effects coursing through our world today. A natural tsunami begins in the hidden world under the sea, and is generated by underwater earthquakes caused by the shift of the earth's tectonic plates. As it travels at great speeds underwater to the shores both near and far, it builds in destructive force, which wreaks great havoc, upon its arrival at those shores.

Likewise, there are hidden events and initiatives being spawned out of our sight, which will culminate in the major destructive events of the end times. This is true especially in the global economy and political arenas where behaviors which will reach fruition in the person of the Antichrist are being spawned.

Warning systems have been in place for millennia. Except for those who have studied biblical prophesies; most of mankind is oblivious to those warnings.

God designed the universe according to His own plan to reward those who serve and obey Him. He also warned of the disvalue of disobedience. Just as there are blessings for obeying God, there are consequences for not conforming to His plan and commands.

For too long mankind has tried God's patience. In our world today we are seeing the ripples of the coming tsunami of consequences. Tsunamis give little advance warning of their imminent arrival. If the world situation continues unabated, as it has, we are in for some tough and yet wonderful times.

The Bible warns of a great falling away of some who currently are believers, but will turn their back on God, as we move closer to the final days. On the other hand, during those final days God will restore His chosen people, the Jews, to faith in massive numbers.

The upcoming spiritual tsunami is being prepared by God, as a means of wrapping up His final plans for His creation. Just as two tectonic plates violently rub together to produce earthquakes, God and Satan are moving to violently oppose one another in the last days. We, who have read the Book, know that God and his followers will come out the winners in this contest.

In current news and media we are seeing the work of the devil in:

- the growing apostasy of believers
- degradation of moral values
- economic chaos

- political intrigues
- unrestrained violence in many regions of the world

Men with antichrist-like qualities are moving both behind the scenes, as well as in the public eye. People with a modicum of biblical knowledge are looking forward to the event known as the *Rapture.*

At the same time we are hearing and seeing reports of tremendous spiritual revival and acceptance of Jesus taking place among people groups previously hardened against the gospel of Jesus the Messiah. In world events, the formation of the coalition involved in the coming war of Gog and Magog is discernible. Nations specifically cited in scripture are forming an alliance, which will come against Israel during the times of the spiritual tsunami.

Remember that no matter how dark the end-time events seem to be, God has it all under control. That's why each chapter ends with the words: **But God** . . . !

Interpretation of Scripture

Hermeneutics is the science and methodology of interpreting texts, especially the books of the Bible. Sound interpretation of scripture requires a consistent application of principles derived by the field of hermeneutics: Context, grammar, and exegesis. Exegesis (i.e. letting scripture itself reveal the true meaning of a passage) differs from its false counterpart; *eisegesis* (i.e. interpreting scripture using as a filter, personal presuppositions and expectations) in that *eisegesis* imposes preconceived ideas and often false understanding on the passage of scripture. Such false preconceptions come in large part from personal desires or societally malformed ideas.

This book will use the above methods of hermeneutics as the primary approach to explaining the convergences of Biblical prophecy and current events.

Tools like Occam's razor, context, literal interpretation, and grammar serve to provide guidelines to aid scripture interpretation.

Occam's Razor

This tool uses a simple technique to keep interpretation on track.

This principle may be plainly stated, "Of several acceptable explanations for a phenomenon, the simplest is preferable, provided that it takes all circumstances into account." [Author's paraphrase].

Popularly, one hears it in what is commonly called the (K.I.S.S.) Principle—Keep it simple [saints]. Don't make it more complicated than it needs to be.

Context

Simply put—***A text out of context is a pretext.***

Literal Interpretation

Avoid reading into a scripture anything more than it says. Unless the language used suggests a metaphorical description is intended by the author, take it as it stands.

Grammar

Use a good concordance or lexicon to gain understanding of the words used. And avoid applying Western civilization understanding to Middle-Eastern concepts. The two are often very different, if not totally opposite.

Current Events

Scripture records prophesy about the period of future history, which is called the end times. Today one must have a Bible in hand, as one reads or hears of current events in the television, print, Internet or broadcast media.

Proof-of-Concept Events

A *proof-of-concept* event is an occurrence previewing the kind of actions described in scripture, but not fully manifested until certain other signal events have happened.

There are events recorded in scripture:

- Drying up of the Euphrates River.
- Food prices expanding exponentially.
- Families falling apart.
- Calls for a one-world government and financial system.
- Formation of a coalition of nations specifically mentioned in the Bible.
- A rising desire for the imminent return of Jesus.

One such event spoken of in the apocalyptic book of Revelation is the drying up of the Euphrates River, in Iraq. Turkey and Syria have placed dams across the Euphrates River, as it passes through their countries dropping the flow rate to almost zero across much of Iraq.

Economic Chaos

Anyone at all aware of the global situation today recognizes that the entire world is economically *circling the drain*. World economies are in a chaotic state with rampant money fluctuations, rising unemployment, pending changes in long-standing financial certainties, etc.

Oil Discoveries in Israel

Scripture speaks of oil in Israel, but until recently, most people thought that was a forlorn hope without substance. Now discoveries of oil and natural gas within the land of Israel are proving that God's Word is true.

Rebuilding of the Ancient City of Babylon

Saddam Hussein began rebuilding the ancient city in 1983 reportedly to link his name to that of the great Babylonian leader, Nebuchadnezzar.[1] Nebuchadnezzar ruled Babylon from 605-562 B.C. and took the two southern Israelite tribes (i.e. Judah and Benjamin) into captivity in 597 B.C.[2] Since Saddam Hussein's execution on December 30, 2006, there are ongoing efforts by *United Nations* (UN) and Iraqi leaders to continue the rebuilding of the ancient city and use it as a tourist attraction.[3] Babylon will play a prominent role during the Tribulation Period.

Moral Decline

As forecast in scripture, the last days will see a decline in morals throughout the world.

Ethical Decline

The darker side of humanity is emerging as ethics are judged against a floating standard. Situational ethics are increasingly being used as a guide to decision-making.

Attacks against Israel

From ancient times, the Promised Land was attacked by Israel's enemies. Some of the major enemies include:

- Amalekites
- Philistines
- Assyria
- Babylon
- Rome

Since the inception of Israel as a modern nation in 1948, Israel has been the object of attacks from her enemies:

- Arab coalition nations attacked
- Suez Canal Conflict

- Six-day War
- Yom Kippur attacks
- War with Lebanon & Hezbollah, which were augmented by 1500 Iranian Revolutionary Guard troops
- First Palestinian Intifada
- Scud missile attacks from Iraq
- Missile attacks from Gaza & Ramallah by Palestinians

Sometime in the future, a Russian (i.e. Magog) coalition, led by a leader called Gog, will attack Israel.

- ????—War of Gog & Magog

Peace in the Middle East

People, for a variety of reasons or motivations, want to see peace in the Middle East:

- Some because they want cheap oil again.
- Some because of personal naiveté want to see a lessening of tensions in the region.
- Others desire unity for religious reasons.

Scripture records that there will be a leader who will enter into a seven-year treaty with Israel and usher in such a peace accord, which will, however, be revoked midway through the seven years.

One World Government

A call for one person or body to govern the world and move to a world money system is growing. Some assert we are no longer just individual nations, but rather a global society. This is a radical shift in thinking from nationalism to globalism. Schools from K through 16 are heavily influencing this shift in thinking. [4]

Apostasy

Scripture warns that in the last days, men and women will allow themselves to be carried away by the error of lawless men and so fall away from faith. People are moving away from the prior religious framework in which their parents were raised.

Persecution of Believers

Where formerly tolerance prevailed in many non-Christian parts of the world as a result of recognition of a generally positive assessment of Christianity, today, native religions opposed to Christian values are increasingly moving their followers to persecute Christians.

Seven Churches of Asia

These seven churches recorded in John's Apocalypse have been examples of how to and also how not to live as believers.

Environmental Disasters

Earthquakes in Chili, Japan, Iran have caused significant destruction. The recent tsunami in Japan following the 8.9 magnitude quake displaced over 400,000 people and killed almost 10,000. Damage to nuclear reactors raised enormous fears of a possible nuclear disaster. A sunspot storm on the sun was of a magnitude sufficient to disable electronics worldwide, if it had been aimed directly toward the earth. We ***are*** experiencing warming of the earth, but not caused solely by humans, as some have mistakenly stated. The warming and cooling of the earth is historically, cyclical in nature, causing the truly uninformed to cry *wolf.*

Science & Technology

The prophet Daniel spoke of the increase of knowledge in the last days (Dan. 12:4).

The Great "Snatching Away"

There is a growing interest and expectation among Biblically literate Christians in the event called *The Rapture or Parousia*. There are a number of theories about the timing of this event, but many Christians have a sense that it is on the horizon.

Coalition of Countries

The Bible records a list of specific countries, which will come against Israel in the last days in the War of Gog and Magog. Those countries are currently forming a coalition of nation-states, which will comprise a major threat to Israel.

Vulture Population on the Increase in Israel

Two wars (i.e. Gog & Magog and Armageddon) in Israel will result in so many dead that normal methods of burial, cremation, etc. will be incapable of handling the casualties. Scripture states that on both occasions, God will have birds of the air complete the work required. The formerly endangered species list includes the Griffin vulture whose population had diminished to dangerous levels. For a time, the Griffin vulture population appeared to be on the increase, but has decreased again somewhat.

Third Temple in Jerusalem

Both Jewish and Christian believers have expressed their passionate desire to see the Temple in Jerusalem rebuilt. Jews are preparing right now to begin construction on the Temple. Furniture and worship implements have already been fabricated, with few exceptions, from descriptions and plans found in scripture.

Second Coming of Christ

Increasingly, Christians are quietly and vocally yearning for the return of Jesus Christ prophesied in scripture.

False Messiahs

While false messiahs have emerged throughout recorded history, today, there appears to be more individuals who claim to fill that role. In Islamic belief, the Mahdi is a prophet or messiah who is expected to appear in the world sometime before it ends. Islam looks forward to the coming return of their Mahdi (the 12th Imam) to fill the role.

Seven Years of Tribulation

Daniel prophesied that there would be a *week* of years (e.g. Daniel's *Seventieth Week*—Dan. 9:26-27) of increasing trouble in the world. The book of Revelation likewise goes into great detail about events, which will take place during those seven years. Some events occurring today are clear precursors to or foreshadowing of events prophesied in scripture for that period.

Armageddon

The great end-time battle, thought by many as being foretold to take place near Megiddo in Israel, is being discussed more and more. Some events have been suggested as embodying such a battle. Questions have been raised asking whether this event or another (e.g. Gog and Magog) can be considered the epic battle.

Thousand Year Period

Following the end of the Tribulation (i.e. including the portion known as the Great Tribulation) will come a thousand year period called the Millennium Period. At the end of this period the world will experience a release of evil again for a brief time, followed by final judgment for mankind.

Final Thoughts

Reading about the end-times is interesting and sometimes scary. Simply acquiring knowledge is insufficient. Action is called for.

Timelines

Timelines depicting various views of end-time events are shown in Appendix A.

End-times timelines with various rapture views are shown in Appendix B.

CHAPTER 1

Proof-of-Concept Events

> [12] *Now we see but a poor reflection as in a mirror; then we shall see face to face. Now I know in part; then I shall know fully, even as I am fully known.* (1 Cor. 13:12 NIV)

A *proof-of-concept* event is an occurrence previewing the kind of actions described in scripture, but not fully manifested until certain other signal events have happened.

There are specific *proof-of-concept* events recorded in scripture that may be seen currently in the world news media:

- Drying up of the Euphrates River (cf. Rev. 16:12).

  One such event spoken of in the apocalyptic book of Revelation is the drying up of the Euphrates River, in Iraq. Turkey and Syria have placed dams across the Euphrates River as it passes through their countries dropping the flow rate to almost zero across much of

Iraq. Funding for a number of these dams came from Russian aid. These phenomena will be discussed more in Chapter 20.

- Food prices expanding exponentially (cf. Rev. 6:1).

Oxfam (i.e. named after the Oxford Committee for Famine Relief, founded in Great Britain in 1942), is an international confederation of 14 organizations working together to find lasting solutions to poverty and injustice. As a core of their efforts, Oxfam follows global food prices and their effect on world hunger and poverty. Their 2011 report found that, "World food prices reached a new historic peak in January 2011." Oxfam reports that:

"Food prices have recently passed the levels reached during the food crisis of 2007-08. People around the world are starting to feel the impact and some countries like Tunisia, Egypt or Algeria are experiencing riots, caused in part by the increasing costs of food. The sudden food price hikes have pushed millions of people in developing countries further into hunger and poverty. And it's not just high prices that are a problem. Prices are unpredictable, meaning that consumers can't rely on a regular price, and producers are unable to plan their investments with certainty." . . . . Since July 2010, prices of many crops have risen dramatically. Prices of maize increased 74%; wheat went up by 84%; sugar by 77% and oils and fats by 57%. Rice prices fortunately remain fairly stable with prices in December 2010 less than 4% higher than the previous year; meat and dairy also remained stable, but at high levels.[1]

This phenomenon will be discussed more in Chapter 20.

- Families falling apart (cf. Matt. 10:34-36).

  Since the revolutionary cultural changes of the 1960s, increasingly, married couples are experiencing or perceiving trauma that causes many to decide to dissolve their unions with the resulting negative impact on family coherence. Children are stressing over the possibility that their family may be next. Some even assume that it is ***normal*** for parents to divorce and lose the children's loyalties. This has created an expectation that marriage may not produce the benefits that were historically expected from a life-long covenant relationship between a man and a woman. These phenomena will be discussed more in Chapter 5.

- Calls for a one-world government and financial system (cf. Rev. 13:3).

  With the chaos of today's world economy, calls for someone to fix the mess will arise globally at some point. Already, the media has reported that people are crying out for resolutions from the United Nations and other world bodies to bring healing to what has been described by some experts as a, *vicious downward* [economic] *spiral* that has emerged following a seemingly *virtuous upward* [economic] *spiral.* From a long period of *laissez les bons moments de rouler* (i.e. let the good times roll), characterized by profligate spending, we have moved to a cry of, *Won't somebody help us out of this mess*! No single segment of society has been able to arrive at a suitable solution for the world's economic and political challenges. This phenomenon will be discussed more in Chapter 9.

- Formation of a coalition of nations specifically mentioned in the Bible (cf. Ezek. 38:1-6).

Ezekiel mentions several countries that will join Russia in a coalition: Persia, Cush, Put, Gomer, Beth Torgarmah, and "the many nations with you" (Ezek. 38:5-6).

- A rising desire for the imminent return of Jesus (cf. 1 Thess. 4:17).

  Jews have looked for the promised Messiah who they expect to come as a conquering king, coming to save them, not realizing that He has already come. Christians are simply looking for the return of Jesus, recognizing that He is the Christ (Messiah).

An additional *proof-of-concept* event recorded in history that is not yet seen in its final manifestation in the world news media currently is,

- Selucid Empire King Antiochus IV Epiphanes entered the 2nd Temple in Jerusalem to defile it. [2]

  He ordered the sacrifice of a pig on the altar, thus foreshadowing "an abomination that causes desolation" prophesied by Daniel. (Dan. 9:27b) The Antichrist will do this in the middle of the Tribulation period after being killed, resurrected and in-filled by Satan.

But God . . . !

PART 1

WORLD ECONOMY

- The world-wide collapse of the economies of many nations provides a peek at the tip-of-the-iceberg of world finance. What we see and prescient financial advisors are reporting is the impending melt-down of finances in the global community.
- Discovery of oil in Israel may well, in future, incentivize nations whose dependence on petroleum products drag down their economies and motivate them to steal control of this resource from Israel.
- The current and future role of spiritual and commercial Babylon will have a definite place in the final events of the last days.

CHAPTER 2

Economic Chaos

> [5] *When the Lamb opened the third seal, I heard the third living creature say, "Come!" I looked, and there before me was a black horse! Its rider was holding a pair of scales in his hand.* [6] *Then I heard what sounded like a voice among the four living creatures, saying, "A quart of wheat for a day's wages, and three quarts of barley for a day's wages, and do not damage the oil and the wine!"* (Rev. 6:5-6 NIV)

The world is again experiencing great economic travail. Some are saying this time it is worse than the Great Depression of 1929.

John the apostle recorded some catastrophic financial events at the opening of the third seal in Revelation 6:5-6:

- extremely high prices for essential foodstuff: wheat and barley
- availability of luxury items: oil and wine

Economic Armageddon

David Jeremiah comments on what secular financial writers described in 2008 as Armageddon.[1] Use of such apocalyptic language is increasingly permeating the media to provide fodder for describing the growing global economy.

William Bonner, and Addison Wiggin, in *Empire of Debt*, wrote:

> Americans . . . believe that houses always go up in price. No cobwebs grow over a real estate office door. No mortgage lender sits by the phone waiting for it to ring. And yet, it is impossible for real estate prices to exceed the rate of GDP growth for very long. This belief will also have to be crushed out, by a long bear market in property. Prices in Rome began a downturn in the year AD 300 or so (this we do not know for a fact, it is just a good guess). They did not stop going down until 1,000 years later . . . in the Renaissance . . . or maybe later. Even as late as the eighteenth century, sheep were grazing where the Forum used to be.
>
> The belief in the American empire—in American cultural, political, social, and economic superiority—must also be crushed out somehow. That is the likely next phase . . . the degenerate stage of empire . . . which could last one hundred years or more.
>
> In summary, the theory we have been teasing out is that politics and markets follow similar cyclical patterns—boom, bust, bubble, and bamboozle. A handful of companies usually take a dominant position in the market; sometimes a single one does. So do a few countries dominate world politics . . . "empires" they are called. The difference between a regular nation and an empire is profound. A regular nation—such as Belgium or Bulgaria—tends its own affairs. An empire

> looks outward, taking on its shoulders the fate of much of the world. An empire is like a bull market. It grows, it develops . . . often it passes into a bubble phase, when people come to believe the most absurd things.
>
> We don't know what stage the American empire has reached . . . but we look around and see so many degenerate and absurd things, we guess: We must be nearer the end than the beginning.[2]

Basically, Bonner and Addison are suggesting that Americans are just not paying enough attention to what is really going on. Their likening the situation of America to an empire is more accurate, if one defines an empire as looking beyond its own borders and economy. High food prices, collapse of several parts of our economy (e.g. housing, banking, and rising unemployment) all contribute to an untenable position which, coupled with global problems of a similar nature, cry out for a global solution and one-world government. We will further discuss the one-world government solution in Chapter 9.

Famine and prohibitive food prices

Oxfam (i.e. The Oxford Committee for Famine Relief, a non-governmental confederation of fourteen organizations started in 1942) presents a bleak picture for 2011 regarding the price and availability of food world-wide.

> Food prices have recently passed the levels reached during the food crisis of 2007-08. People around the world are starting to feel the impact and some countries like Tunisia, Egypt or Algeria are experiencing riots, caused in part by the increasing costs of food. The sudden food price hikes have pushed millions of people in developing countries further into hunger and poverty. And it's not just high prices that are a problem. Prices are unpredictable, meaning that

> consumers can't rely on a regular price, and producers are unable to plan their investments with certainty. [3]

While the current events are not precisely those spoken of in Revelation at the opening of the third seal, they are clearly of the category we have defined as "proof of concept." Recent riots in Tunisia, Egypt, Albania, Syria, Israel and Jordan at least partially underscore the effect that instability in food supplies and prices are likely to produce an outcry for some sort of world government to help manage and smooth out economic fluctuations.

Got Questions.org responded to a question about Biblical prophecy and a one-world-government or one-world-currency with the following caution: "The Bible does not use the phrase 'one-world government' or 'one-world currency' in referring to the end times. It does, however, provide ample evidence to enable us to draw the conclusion that both will exist under the rule of the Antichrist in the last days.[4]

Time magazine reported in late 1974 on man's struggle for food through the ages:

> Nothing is older to man than his struggle for food. From the time the early hunters stalked the mammoths and the first sedentary "farmers" scratched the soil to coax scrawny grain to grow, man has battled hunger. History is replete with his failures. The Bible chronicles one famine after another; food was in such short supply in ancient Athens that visiting ships had to share their stores with the city; Romans prayed at the threshold of Olympus for food.
>
> Every generation in medieval Europe suffered famine. The poor ate cats, dogs and the droppings of birds; some starving mothers ate their children. In the 20th century, periods of extreme hunger drove Soviet citizens to cannibalism, and as late as 1943, floods destroyed so much of Bengal's crops that deaths from starvation reached the millions. [5]

The Judeo-Christian scriptures tell of a time of famine in Egypt in which Joseph bar Jacob administered Egyptian crops for the Pharaoh enabling Joseph to bless Jews fleeing that same famine in Judea (Gen. 41:1-49). Pharaoh had a dream and sent for Joseph to interpret it because Joseph, with God's insight, had successfully interpreted an earlier dream for him. Because of Joseph's perspicacity, Pharaoh put Joseph in charge of administering the country's resources in preparation for the famine.

The famine was region-wide; affecting even Joseph's family in Israel, and resulting in their moving to Egypt under the Pharaoh's sponsorship.

One might inquire in what way famine events affect the world's economy. Famine in any part of the world places additional burden on the remaining parts of the world to produce enough food for themselves and those impacted by the lack of food.

Famine may result from natural events, the devastation of human conflict, poor management of food resources, or from unchecked population growth. All of these exist in the world today.

Natural events such as drought, tsunamis, tornados, fire, and flood may all contribute to a lower (i.e. or lack of) production of food. The destruction brought by wars, coupled with diversion of productive farmers to the task of war rather than production of food will also contribute to the conditions bringing on famine. Even when foodstuffs are available, government or ruling leadership in a region may divert food provided by more charitable or more prosperous regions to their own use or misuse. While some nations are attempting to curb their exploding populations, (e.g. China, a prime example with their one-child-per-family rule), others are using population growth to promote their religious goals. Islam is a good example with an approach to global jihad based upon growing their presence in non-Muslim countries.

All of these situations exist in the world today as a direct illustration of the consequences of Paul's warning to Timothy in 2 Timothy 3:1-5

(New International Version) about the mind-set of people in the last days:

"People will be:

- lovers of themselves
- lovers of money
- boastful
- proud
- abusive
- disobedient to their parents
- ungrateful
- unholy
- without love
- unforgiving
- slanderous
- without self-control
- brutal
- not lovers of the good
- treacherous
- rash
- conceited lovers of pleasure rather than lovers of God
- having a form of godliness but denying its power"

All of this contributes to the conditions, which will result in famine in various places of the world—now and particularly in the last days.

Recession and Depression

Economic policies since the 1990s and have contributed to the major economic downturn in global finances. Countries are nearing bankruptcy and would go bankrupt if they were not bailed out by other nations. Greece, Spain, the United States and France are all experiencing significant downturns in their economies. If they had not had their debts guaranteed by other nations who purchased their bonds, bankruptcy would have resulted, if they had been corporations.

But because currencies may be shored up by printing new money and selling bonds to other nations, bankruptcy is usually forestalled.

Most people are aware of the easing of loan requirements authored by the *United States* (U.S.) government in the '90s and ill-advised legislation that required banks to accept sub-prime loans. 20-20 hindsight now reveals that, *whoops, we really blew that one.* In a time of growing world economic strength and prosperity, it was enticing to think that things would always get better financially. Basically, we began *to eat our seed corn.* Every farmer knows that you must retain a portion of your crops as seed for the next growing season.

Policies set by governments have ignored this fact. Restricting drilling for oil on the flimsy excuse of placating environmental activists and legislating unrealistic laws *to feather the nests* of special interest groups are destroying the viability of the world economy. This does not mean that mankind should not regulate initiatives or activities that damage the world ecology. However, imputing human rights onto the animal or vegetable kingdom is just plain ignorant and counter to God's design. Some activists would have man defer to the insect or animal kingdom for the right to live on this planet. They forget that when God created the earth, he said,

> . . . "Be fruitful and increase in number, fill the earth and subdue it. Rule over the fish of the sea and the birds of the air and over every living creature that moves on the ground." Then God said, "I give you every seed-bearing plant on the face of the whole earth and every tree that has fruit with seed in it. They will be yours for food. And to all the beasts of the earth and all the birds of the air and all the creatures that move on the ground—everything that has the breath of life in it—I give every green plant for food." . . . (Gen. 1:28-30 NIV)

The global economy was bolstered by the greed of the banks, corporations, and politicians *out to get their piece of the pie.*

Economists are currently mixed on declaring the world situation as either a recession or an actual depression.

Unemployment

The United States (U.S.) government unemployment as reported in the media is understated because they published numbers that ignore people who have given up seeking employment. The following are not considered part of the workforce:

1. Persons Under 16
2. Inmates
3. Non-Civilian Population (Armed Forces)
4. Persons who do not have jobs, and who have not been actively seeking work in the prior 4 weeks.

According to Donald Trump and Robert Kiyosaki, authors of *Midas Touch: Why Some Entrepreneurs Get Rich—And Why Most Don't*, in an October 7, 2011 interview on Newsmax TV:

> The nation's [U.S.] unemployment rate is significantly higher than stated in the government's monthly tallies and the number of jobless citizens is now approaching levels not seen since the Great Depression . . . *The sad thing is unemployment is really probably at 21 percent if you go by the real numbers*, Trump said. *When you say 9.1 . . . that number is not a real number, the real number is 21 percent and it could even be higher than that.* [6]
>
> Other world economies are much worse off than the United States. The highest reported unemployment rate is Namibia at 51.2%. Nations above 20% include: Rwanda (30%); South Africa (25%); Angola (25%); Spain (21.5%); and Nigeria (21.1%). [7]

Bubbles a'pop'in

Economist David Weidmer, in his book, *Aftershook*, describes the result of several *bubbles* that have and are contributing to the current collapse of the world economies. Weidmer began writing about *bubbles* in 2006 in his first book, *America's Bubble Economy*, the following areas which came after the Dot-com bubble crash of the 1990s:

- real estate
- stock market
- private debt
- discretionary spending
- dollar
- government debt [8]

He and his co-authors predicted in 2008 that within two-three years the multiple bubbles would begin to decline and eventually burst because they were based on unsustainable growth in each of the sectors above.

Newsmax reported on a dire prediction of Sir John Templeton written before his death in July of 2008. Christopher Ruddy, CEO & Editor in Chief of *Newsmax* and *Moneynews*, reported:

> Sir John had accurately predicted the dot-com crash of 2000 and 2001. When I met him again for the last time in December of 2004, he was warning that the housing bubble would eventually crash, with home prices falling by as much as 50 percent or more from their highs in some markets . . . He predicted a fall-off of the stock market after that . . . Both predictions were not widely accepted at the time, yet they eventually came to pass . . . In his last memorandum on the markets and the economy, he elaborated on these same themes, warning of dire economic "chaos"—which he predicted would last many years . . . Still, he was optimistic on equity investments, specifically

> in globally diverse companies with high growth patterns and wide profit margins.

Ruddy goes on to say, "In June of 2005, Sir John penned a memorandum to friends and family that is uncanny and prophetic in its vision of what would happen to the U.S. and global economy:"

> Financial Chaos—probably in many nations in the next five years. The word chaos is chosen to express likelihood of reduced profit margin at the same time as acceleration in cost of living . . . Mortgages and other forms of debts are over tenfold greater now than ever before 1970, which can cause manifold increases in bankruptcy auctions . . . Most of the methods of universities and other schools which require residence have become hopelessly obsolete. Probably over half of the universities in the world will disappear quickly over the next thirty years . . . Obsolescence is likely to have a devastating effect in a wide variety of human activities, especially in those where advancement is hindered by labor unions or other bureaucracies or by government regulations . . . Accelerating competition is likely to cause profit margins to continue to decrease and even become negative in various industries. Over tenfold more persons hopelessly indebted leads to multiplying bankruptcies not only for them but for many businesses that extend credit without collateral. Voters are likely to enact rescue subsidies, which transfer the debts to governments, such as Fannie May and Freddie Mac . . . Comparisons show that prosperity flows toward those nations having most freedom of competition.
>
> In this memo, Templeton shows a remarkable degree of prescience about the direction that the American economy [soon to be followed by the European economy] was taking. [9]

With the direction world economies are moving, it should not come as a surprise that people will begin to call for someone to lead in a recovery. Individual governments or even groups of governments, such as the European Union will demonstrate their inadequacy to accomplish the complex path to recovery. This will result in increased cry for a one-world leader and one-world government, setting the stage for the arrival of the Antichrist.

The real estate and stock market bubbles have burst. The discretionary spending bubble has burst and people are realigning their consumer spending habits to reflect it with the attendant loss of jobs in the consumer products sector. People are making things last longer and surprisingly, buying consumer goods of a higher quality with the expectation of the products lasting longer.

In 1943, Abraham Maslow introduced the concept of a hierarchy of needs experienced by people. Maslow wrote about what he saw as needs:

- physiological (e.g. lowest)
- security
- social
- esteem
- self-actualizing (e.g. highest)

Without *getting down in the weeds* of a technical discussion about Maslow's original hierarchy and a later revision, which reflects new findings and theory from fields like neuroscience, developmental psychology and evolutionary psychology, it is sufficient to say; satisfaction of one level of need does not necessarily move one beyond it. Each level of need remains a need among all the other stages of need.

People are motivated to fulfill basic physiological needs before addressing higher needs: food, sleep, air, and water are the basic needs for humans and tend to move people to seek fulfillment of them first.

Whenever economies falter, unemployment rises, lower income people find purchasing food harder and are moved to seek satisfaction of the basic needs first by simply purchasing fewer or lower-quality products. As the economy declines, some may have greater difficulty buying sufficient foodstuffs to stay alive, leading ultimately to famine conditions.

Whatever events have been in place to force people to seek the more basic needs first may include:

- war
- environmental disasters
- disease
- poor governance (economy, corruption, politics, transportation infrastructure inadequacy/failure, leader's greed, misuse of natural resources)
- population growth

All of these are happening today somewhere in the world. The first three especially characterize the last days as related by the Apostle Matthew in Matt. 24 and by the Apostle John in Revelation during the seven-year Tribulation period.

Most economists agree that the global economy is at its most chaotic in recent memory.

Return of a Technological Bubble

In the midst of the web bubble excitement, a cautionary note was struck by the *Economist* warning of a bubble-burst—"Irrational exuberance has returned to the internet world. Investors should beware." the *Economist* article discusses the impact of unwise support of the tech bubble by "angels" who artificially inflate the market:

> So is history indeed about to repeat itself? . . . [T]he tech landscape has changed dramatically since the late 1990s . . . . [T]oday there are 2 billion netizens, many of them in huge

new wired markets such as China. A dozen years ago ultra-fast broadband connections were rare; today they are ubiquitous. And last time many start-ups (remember Webvan and Pets.com) had massive ambitions but puny revenues; today web stars such as Groupon, which offers its users online coupons, and Zynga, a social-gaming company, have phenomenal sales and already make respectable profits.

The this-time-it's-different brigade also points out that the 1990s bubble expanded only after numerous web firms were floated on stock markets and naive investors pumped up the price of their shares to insane levels. This time, there have been relatively few big internet IPOs (though that is likely to change) . . . . In one respect the optimists are right. This time is indeed different, though not because the boom-and-bust cycle has miraculously disappeared. It is different because the tech bubble-in-the-making is forming largely out of sight in private markets and has a global dimension that its predecessor lacked . . . . The bubble is being pumped partly by wealthy "angel" investors, some of whom made their fortunes in the late-1990s IPO boom . . . . This boom also has wider horizons than the previous one. It was arguably started by Russian investors. Skype was born in Estonia. Finland's Rovio, which makes the popular Angry Birds smartphone game, recently raised $42m. And then there's China. Renren and Youku, "China's YouTube", supposedly offer investors a chance to profit both from the country's extraordinary growth and from the broader impact of the internet on commerce and society. Chinese web start-ups often command $15m-20m valuations in early financing rounds, far more than their peers in America . . . . These differences will have important consequences. The first is that the bubble forming in the private market could be pretty big by the time it floats into the public one. [10]

In May 2011, the successful launch of the LinkedIn *Initial Public Offering* (IPO) produced an excitement about tech stocks that emerged in the midst of a number of Silicon Valley initiatives: LinkedIn (IPO), Groupon (IPO), and Microsoft's acquisition of Skype. The *Wall Street Journal* reported on the excitement generated by the LinkedIn (IPO):

> Silicon Valley's technology frenzy burst onto the stock market Thursday as LinkedIn Corp.'s shares more than doubled in their first day of trading, setting the stage for debuts from other Internet companies such as Facebook Inc. and Groupon Inc . . . . The outsize demand for the stock of an Internet company that is growing rapidly but had a profit of $15.4 million last year is the latest sign of the surge—some say bubble—in Web valuations even as the broader U.S. economy struggles to rebound from the recession. [11]

Those manipulating the markets for their own enrichment may find themselves at odds with the global financial picture and also, more importantly with God's plan for the end times. "The LORD foils the plans of the nations; he thwarts the purposes of the peoples. But the plans of the LORD stand firm forever, the purposes of his heart through all generations" (Psa. 33:10-11).

Housing Bubble

Home prices are expected to experience a *triple dip* by June 2012. Fiserv, a technology provider for financial services, is forecasting that "home values are expected to fall another 3.6% by next June, pushing them to a new low of 35% below the peak reached in early 2006 and marking a triple dip in prices." Two of the factors driving home values lower include the rising number of foreclosed properties that lenders are placing back on the market and the rising number of homes still awaiting foreclosure processing that will be put on the market by mid-year 2012.

Triple Dip refers to the third drop in home values since 2009 when the first post-bubble bottom hit and prices fell to 31% below peak. The second drop took place in the winter of 2010 with the expiration of the artificial First-Time Buyer credit, dropping prices to 33% below their former peak. The anticipated third dip in home values will likely result from the re-insertion of the current inventory of foreclosed homes into the housing market. [12]

Cry for a Global Economy

The impact of the current economic chaos is a growing cry for a global economy. The Vatican is even getting into the act and recommending:

> . . . [T]he establishment of "a supranational authority" with worldwide scope and "universal jurisdiction" to guide economic policies and decisions . . . Such an authority should start with the United Nations as its reference point but later become independent and be endowed with the power to see to it that developed countries were not allowed to wield "excessive power over the weaker countries". [13]

Occupy Wall Street Movement

The October 22, 2011 issue of the *Economist* reported:

> From Seattle to Sydney, protesters have taken to the streets. Whether they are inspired by the Occupy Wall Street movement in New York or by the indignados in Madrid, they burn with dissatisfaction about the state of the economy, about the unfair way that the poor are paying for the sins of rich bankers, and in some cases about capitalism itself. [14]

In another article in the October 22, 2011 issue, *The Economist* discussed the protests and suggested a possible response:

> If the grievances are more legitimate and broader than previous rages against the machine, then the dangers are also greater. Populist anger, especially if it has no coherent agenda, can go anywhere in times of want . . . . [Brave] politicians would focus on two things. The first is tackling the causes of the rage speedily. Above all that means doing more to get their economies moving again . . . . Reform finance vigorously . . . . The second is telling the truth—especially about what went wrong. The biggest danger is that legitimate criticisms of the excesses of finance risk turning into an unwarranted assault on the whole of globalization [sp]. [15]

A movement among many, predominantly young, people is taking place around the world. Currently as of this writing, protests have mushroomed in over 900 cities in 80-plus countries as reported in the *Economist.* The protests are primarily consensus-based seemingly without an agenda, yet centered on the theme that the capitalist system has denied and ignored the many needs of the poor in the world.

Participants hide behind a somewhat amorphous ignorance that expresses itself in the speaking and sometimes shouting of often inane slogans rather than a coherent call for change. There is a call for change, but no clear description of what that change might look like—except for the destruction of the ***perceived*** stranglehold the world's financiers and capitalists have on the necessary resources to fund supplies for the poor and needy of the world.

Steve Chapman opined in a *Chicago Tribune* article:

> What the movement is getting wrong can be traced to the belief is that the rich have improved their lot by taking money from the not so rich—that wealth has been cruelly redistributed upward. What they overlook is that the real gains come from the creation of new wealth. . . . The

> wealthy are far better off than they used to be. But their improvement has not come at the expense of those down the economic ladder. . . . Not that everything is copacetic. The Great Recession has wrought havoc on the middle class and the poor—eliminating jobs, reducing income and slashing the value of homes. . . . The miserable reality today is not that the many are doing worse because our capitalist system is set up to fleece them for the benefit of the few. They are doing worse because the economy went through a cataclysm from which it has yet to recover. . . . At moments like this, it's not surprising that many Americans would resent the wealthy and feel the urge to punish them. But the OWS demand for action against them is the equivalent of honking your horn when you're stuck in a traffic jam. It makes a lot of noise, without getting you anywhere.[16]

The movement began in Spain in the spring of 2011 and has now spread to 80-plus countries as previously mentioned. The demands of the protestors seem to center on somewhat of a Robin Hood ethos—take from the rich and give to the poor. There is a strong element of socialism (i.e. outright Communism) attached to the movement.

Technology has fueled this movement in much the same way as the Arab Spring movement in Islamic nations, although with a slightly different purpose. The Arab Spring movement was used to overthrow despotic regimes. The Occupy Wall Street movement is attempting to overthrow the capitalist system. YouTube, Twitter, and such have been used to spread the word about the movement's activities and protest locations.

Worldwide Debt

An article in *Moneynews* reported:

> The United States has joined the rogue's gallery of nations whose debt has exceeded its annual economic output, or

> gross domestic product (GDP). The U.S. national debt has broken $15.033 trillion, higher than the $15.032 trillion gross domestic product, meaning as of now, the country's debts are higher than its annual output, according to usdebtclock.org, citing government data.
>
> That's serious, says Gennaro Bernile, a professor of finance at the University of Miami. "The message is very simple: the minute that the debt becomes as large as GDP, GDP has to start growing more than the interest that the U.S. pays in order to keep up with the debt." That's just to break even and assuming the U.S. doesn't get dragged back into another recession.
>
> "If the debt and the GDP are at the same level, and with the debt you have to pay interest at 1 percent, that means that next year the growth in GDP has to be at least 1 percent to keep just with the interest payments," Bernile adds. Like in Europe, U.S. policymakers must decide what steps to take to reduce debt burdens, as tough austerity measures often lead to reduced government, and reduced government leads to reduced public-sector payrolls, and that means less tax revenues going back into the Treasury. [17]

The worldwide debt picture is not good and could develop into a worldwide recession or depression if not improved. [Note: figures were not available for China.] Global debt of large economies compared to each country's *Gross Domestic Product* (GDP) is, as of this writing: [18]

	GDP (in U.S. Dollars)	Foreign Debt to GDP	Foreign Debt (in U.S. Dollars)	Govt Debt to GDP	Risk Status
US	$14.46 Trillion	101%	$14.59 Trillion	100%	Low
France	$2.41 Trillion	235%	$ 5.62 Trillion	87%	Medium
Spain	$0.94 Trillion	284%	$2.54 Trillion	67%	Medium
Portugal	$0.27 Trillion	251%	$0.54 Trillion	106%	High
Italy	$1.2 Trillion	163%	$2.68 Trillion	121%	High
Ireland	$0.27 Trillion	1093%	$2.28 Trillion	109%	High
Greece	$0.27 Trillion	252%	$0.54 Trillion	166%	High
Japan	$5.49 Trillion	50%	$2.68 Trillion	233%	Low
Germany	$3.21 Trillion	176%	$5.62 Trillion	83%	Low
UK	2.28 Trillion	436%	$9.77 Trillion	81%	Low

Global Efforts

A French 24 Hour international news article reported:

> The world's major central banks are joining forces to work together to lower borrowing costs for foreign banks, in a bid to temper the Euro zone's deepening debt crisis. . . .The surprise emergency move by the U.S. Federal Reserve, the European Central Bank, the Bank of Japan and the central banks of Britain, Canada and Switzerland recalled coordinated action to steady global markets in the 2008 financial crisis.

> The euro and European shares surged on the news, which came after euro zone finance ministers agreed to ramp up the firepower of their bailout fund but acknowledged they may have to turn to the International Monetary Fund for more help.[19]

The *Los Angeles Times* reported on the same story:

> Reacting to the deepening Eurozone debt crisis, the Federal Reserve and five other major central banks joined forces Wednesday to offer European lenders easier access to dollars in an attempt to quell growing fears of a global funding crunch.
>
> The Fed said its coordinated action with the European Central Bank, the Bank of Japan and three others was intended to "ease strains in financial markets" and mitigate the resulting effects of a credit squeeze for businesses and households.
>
> The announcement gave an immediate lift to European markets, and U.S. stock futures surged.
>
> The action, which follows a similar coordinated move in September, lowers the cost of so-called dollar swap lines to increase the flow of cash to European lenders. The new pricing would take affect next Monday.[20]

Moving on . . .

In Part 2, we will discuss the moral and ethical decline that is marking many parts of the world culture today and will increasingly impact global economies as the end times grow closer.

But God . . . !

CHAPTER 3

Oil Discoveries In Israel

> [24] *About Asher he said: "Most blessed of sons is Asher; let him be favored by his brothers, and let him bathe his feet in oil."* (Deut. 33:24 NIV)
>
> [22] *"Joseph is a fruitful vine . . . near a spring . . . blessings of the heavens above, blessings of the deep that lies below . . . Let all these rest on the head of Joseph, on the brow of the prince among his brothers."*
>
> (Gen. 49:22-26 NIV)

Scripture speaks of oil in Israel, but until recently, most people thought that was a forlorn hope without substance. Now discoveries of oil and natural gas within the land of Israel are proving that God's Word is true.

A *Ynet* article published in August 2010 ran with the headline, "1.5 billion barrels of oil discovered near Rosh Ha'Ayin." [1]

Israel has been looking for oil under its soil since shortly after its renewal as a state in 1948. *Wall Street Journal* archives reveal the following headlines:

- 1955—"Discovery of Oil Is Announced by Israel"
- 1977—"Israel Discovers Oil in the Gulf of Suez after Eight Failures" (Could be forced to give it to Egypt)
- 1978—"Israel Could Be One of First Countries to Feel the Effects of Iranian Oil Strike"
- 1979—"Israel, Facing Oil Cutoff, Rushes to Develop Field"
- 2010—"Big Gas Find Sparks A Frenzy In Israel"

Legend has it that Prime Minister Golda Meir once ruefully quipped, "Let me tell you something we Israelis have against Moses. He took us forty years into the desert in order to bring us to the one place in the Middle East that has no oil."

Yet God has given the nation of Israel abundant supplies of oil. A number of scriptures record God's provision for His chosen people:

- Genesis 49:1, 22-26 cites "blessings of the deep that lies below" for Joseph and his offspring.
- Deuteronomy 32:9-13 speaks of "nourish[ing]" Jacob with "honey from the rock and oil from the flinty crag"
- Deuteronomy 33:13, 19, 24 says Asher will "bathe his feet in oil."

The Meged 5 oil field reported on in the previously cited article in Ynet News is expected to contain 1.5 billion barrels of oil. Givot Olam, the developer, is hopeful that production will demonstrate that Meged 5 is a commercially viable oil field. While some seem to have doubts, God has made promises to the Israeli people that will be fulfilled. Givot Olam is a privately held company started by religious Jews. In 1988, Tovia Luskin, a Russian Jew from Sidney, Australia sought the prayers of a Lubavitcher Rebbe (Lubavich Chabad, an ultra-conservative Jewish sect, rabbi) in New York for success in an Oil Drilling venture in Israel based on scriptural references to the presence of oil in Israel. [2]

CBN News reported in a May 2010 article based on a broadcast interview that same month that John Brown, the founder of Zion Oil and Gas in Texas, based his intended oil exploration in Israel on Biblical references to oil in Israel. Brown stated that he began his company and his 30-year-old mission to find oil in Israel. The article reported: [3]

> [O]ne company believes there is plenty of oil in the Holy Land and they intend to find it. A potential discovery could change the dynamics of the Middle East and Israel's future . . . John Brown is the founder of Zion Oil and Gas. He started the company on what he said is a God-given, 30-year-old mission to discover oil in Israel . . . . "I was an alcoholic and God saved me and delivered me from alcohol," Brown said. "That was in '81. Jim Spillman came to the church that God took me to in Clausen, Mich. And Jim Spillman—that was before the book the Great Treasure Hunt was written—he explained to the congregation that there was oil in Israel and it was in the Bible. That absolutely amazed me." . . . . "We like to say it's the geology confirming the theology," he said.
>
> In June 2010, the *Jerusalem Post* reported that a gas find in the Levant off the western coast of Israel has enough gas to make Israel energy independent and possibly even an exporter of its excess capacity. The expectation of production from the *Leviathan* and *Tamar* fields in the Levant is that they will supply Israel's needs for the next 50-70 years. [4]

If all turns out as expected, Israel will reverse its current energy import status and become a net energy exporter. This may be one of the triggers which will draw additional attention to Israel and place her more at risk for invasion by less energy-rich countries or even by countries jealous of the new resources.

Recovery of the petroleum assets will depend on a level of regional peace which will allow it.

But God . . . !

CHAPTER 4

City of Babylon

> [8] *A second angel followed and said, "Fallen! Fallen is Babylon the Great, which made all the nations drink the maddening wine of her adulteries."*
>
> *(Rev. 14:8 NIV)*

Saddam Hussein's focus on the rebuilding of Babylon was introduced earlier in this book as was the subsequent interest of other world groups in restoring the ancient city. [1]

Both Ezekiel and Revelation record the significant part which the physical city of Babylon plays in the end times as:

- seat of the world ruler
- center of commerce
- place of beauty
- spiritual center

To be such, Babylon must exist on its ancient site and be afforded the trappings described in scripture. Currently, Iraqi State Board of

Antiquities, the United States, *United Nations Educational, Scientific and Cultural Organization* (UNESCO) and other world agencies are planning to restore and/or rebuild Babylon, as a major cultural attraction without the Saddam Hussein aggrandizing touch. Their goal is to recreate a site, which honors the history and contributions of a great empire.

In a *Stars and Stripes* article, a military newspaper, cited by Joel Rosenberg in his weblog on June 29, 2009, Seth Robinson reported:

> Hillah, Iraq—the remains of what was once the greatest city in the world occupy a vast site on the bank of the Euphrates River.
>
> Their roots go back 3,800 years to when the city of Babylon was the heart of a Mesopotamian empire, and the remnants include great slabs of stone that are said to be the remains of King Nebuchadnezzar's castle. A giant stone lion guards one end of the fortifications, but the most stunning remnants were removed by European archaeologists in the early 20th century.
>
> Now the rapidly improving security situation in [the] surrounding Babil province has persuaded the U.S. State Department and the Iraqi State Board of Antiquities and Heritage to embark on the preservation project, dubbed the Future of Babylon Project.
>
> The State Department and the World Monuments Fund have committed $700,000 to the project, which will see U.S. and Iraqi experts develop a plan to preserve the site and develop a local tourism industry, said Diane Siebrandt, the U.S. embassy's cultural heritage officer.
>
> The Babylon project is one of several that the State Department is involved in to conserve ancient sites in partnership with the Iraqi government, she said. [2]

As mentioned previously, prior to his death by hanging in December 2006, Saddam Hussein had developed plans and had begun the restoration of Babylon to something of its former glory. Until the intervention of armed conflict with the United States, Hussein had intended to commission the rebuilding of the famed Hanging Gardens that were listed, as one of the seven wonders of the ancient world. So, what does this have to do with biblical prophecy about the end times?

Scripture records succinctly that Babylon will play a central role as a religious, political and economic center during those times.

In Revelation chapter 17, John records that the Woman on the Beast, identified as Mystery Babylon the Great and the Abomination of the Earth, was seated on a beast "Covered with blasphemous names . . . She held a cup in her hand, filled with abominable things . . ." Reference to *blasphemous* and *abominable* things indicates a religious connection. (Rev. 17:3-5)

Political power is recorded also in Revelation 17, where John describes the power granted to Mystery Babylon embodied in the beast which she rides:

> [3] Then the angel carried me away in the Spirit into a desert. There I saw a woman sitting on a scarlet beast that was covered with blasphemous names and had seven heads and ten horns . . . [9] "This calls for a mind with wisdom. The seven heads are seven hills on which the woman sits. [10] They are also seven kings. Five have fallen, one is, the other has not yet come; but when he does come, he must remain for a little while. [11] The beast who once was, and now is not, is an eighth king. He belongs to the seven and is going to his destruction. [12] "The ten horns you saw are ten kings who have not yet received a kingdom, but who for one hour will receive authority as kings along with the beast. [13] They have one purpose and will give their power and authority to the beast. (Rev. 17:3, 9-13 NIV)

The tremendous economic impact affected by Babylon is described in Revelation 18 in the lamentation and loss that will be experienced by the world at her destruction:

> 1 After this I saw another angel coming down from heaven. He had great authority, and the earth was illuminated by his splendor. 2 With a mighty voice he shouted: "Fallen! Fallen is Babylon the Great! She has become a home for demons and a haunt for every evil spirit, a haunt for every unclean and detestable bird. 3 For all the nations have drunk the maddening wine of her adulteries. The kings of the earth committed adultery with her, and the merchants of the earth grew rich from her excessive luxuries." . . . 8 Therefore in one day her plagues will overtake her: death, mourning and famine. She will be consumed by fire, for mighty is the Lord God who judges her. 9 "When the kings of the earth who committed adultery with her and shared her luxury see the smoke of her burning, they will weep and mourn over her. 10 Terrified at her torment, they will stand far off and cry: "'Woe! Woe, O great city, O Babylon, city of power! In one hour your doom has come!' 11 "The merchants of the earth will weep and mourn over her because no one buys their cargoes any more—12 cargoes of gold, silver, precious stones and pearls; fine linen, purple, silk and scarlet cloth; every sort of citron wood, and articles of every kind made of ivory, costly wood, bronze, iron and marble; 13 cargoes of cinnamon and spice, of incense, myrrh and frankincense, of wine and olive oil, of fine flour and wheat; cattle and sheep; horses and carriages; and bodies and souls of men. 14 "They will say, 'The fruit you longed for is gone from you. All your riches and splendor have vanished, never to be recovered.' 15 The merchants who sold these things and gained their wealth from her will stand far off, terrified at her torment. They will weep and mourn 16 and cry out:

> "'Woe Woe, O great city, dressed in fine linen, purple and scarlet, and glittering with gold, precious stones and pearls! [17] In one hour such great wealth has been brought to ruin!' "Every sea captain, and all who travel by ship, the sailors, and all who earn their living from the sea, will stand far off. [18] When they see the smoke of her burning, they will exclaim, 'Was there ever a city like this great city?' [19] They will throw dust on their heads, and with weeping and mourning cry out: "'Woe! Woe, O great city, where all who had ships on the sea became rich through her wealth! In one hour she has been brought to ruin! (Rev. 18:1-3, 8-19 NIV)

There will be much weeping and wailing over the demise of Babylon by:

- all the nations
- kings of the earth
- merchants of the earth
- sea captains
- sailors

Following the Iraq war, corporations and developers are standing by to partner with Iraq to profit from oil and tourism.

The modern nation of Iraq, so recently war-torn is poised for prosperity. In 2009, Joel Rosenberg reported the following:

> Exxon Mobil, the world's largest company, for example, is positioning itself to become a major investor in the Iraqi energy sector. Other major oil companies are doing the same. The Iraqi government in recent months has been developing investment incentive packages to draw in such companies. This week, in fact, such energy companies will actually begin bidding for licenses to develop Iraq's immense but badly atrophied oil exploration, drilling, and

> refining industry. Consider this morning's headline from the Associated Press: "World's big oil companies prepare for return to Iraq." [3]

In the end times, Babylon will become one of the major economic engines of the government of the Antichrist. While this may seem a stretch, given its condition in 2011, events are beginning to emerge on the world scene, which will culminate in this very thing. Pieces are being moved to the board (as in a chess game) now that will result in Messiah's final victory over Satan and his minions—including the revealed Antichrist and his False Prophet.

But God . . . !

PART 2

MORALITY & ETHICS

- Moral decline has been increasing at a faster rate each year for the past sixty years.
- Ethical decline is also increasing in business, education, politics, and religion.

CHAPTER 5

Moral Decline

> *1 But mark this: There will be terrible times in*
> *the last days. 2 People will be lovers of*
> *themselves, lovers of money, boastful, proud,*
> *abusive, disobedient to their parents,*
> *ungrateful, unholy, 3 without love,*
> *unforgiving, slanderous, without self-control,*
> *brutal, not lovers of the good, 4 treacherous,*
> *rash, conceited, lovers of pleasure rather than*
> *lovers of God— 5 having a form of godliness but*
> *denying its power. Have nothing to do with*
> *them.* (2 Tim. 3:1-5 NIV)

As forecasted in scripture, the last days will see a decline in morals throughout the world.

To be moral has to do with conformity to behavioral standards set by the society in which the standards are established. The *Collins English Dictionary* defines *moral* as: [1]

- adhering to conventionally accepted standards of conduct (i.e. adjectival form)
- principles of behavior in accordance with standards of right and wrong (i.e. nominal form)

Will Durant, in *Our Oriental Heritage*, provides insight into the moral development of societal cultures:

> Since no society can exist without order, and no order without regulation, we may take it as a rule of history that the power of custom varies inversely as the multiplicity of laws, much as the power of instinct varies inversely as the multiplicity of thoughts. Some rules are necessary for the game of life; they may differ in different groups, but within the group they must be essentially the same.
>
> These rules may be:
>
> - conventions
> - customs
> - morals
> - laws
>
> Conventions are forms of behavior found expedient by a people; customs are conventions accepted by successive generations, after natural selection through trial and error and elimination; morals are such customs as the group considers vital to its welfare and development. In primitive societies, where there is no written law, these vital customs or morals regulate every sphere of human existence, and give stability and continuity to the social order. Through the slow magic of time such customs, by long repetition, become a second nature in the individual; if he violates them he feels a certain fear, discomfort or shame; this is the origin of that conscience, or moral sense, which Darwin chose as the most impressive distinction between

> animals and men. In its higher development conscience is social consciousness—the feeling of the individual that he belongs to a group, and owes it some measure of loyalty and consideration. Morality is the cooperation of the part with the whole, and of each group with some larger whole. Civilization, of course, would be impossible without it. [2]

Two kinds of standards set limits on a person's conduct: mankind's and God's. Man's standards, embodied in human society and flawed as a result of failing to obey God, provide guidelines for behavior stem from a sometimes warped manner of reasoning. God's standards derive from His perfect plan for mankind.

Over three millennia ago, God set standards for our work and personal relationships and had them recorded in scripture. These seem somewhat rarely followed in the world today:

- love God above all (Deut. 6:5)
- love your neighbor as yourself (Lev. 19:18)
- treat others, as you want to be treated (Matt. 7:12)

Since the historical event known as *The Fall* recounted in Genesis 3, mankind has strayed from the Creator's plans. The moral standards of many societies have born little resemblance to Biblical standards. Those societies remained weak, divisive, and poor. Disease, famine, internal discord, attacks from enemies, immorality and depravity of all sorts have marked those societies as they attempted to live life their own way in contravention to God's way.

Contrary to what our culture teaches us, scripture encourages us to set our hearts and minds on Christ. David Jeremiah has it right when he says, "When we set our heart on something, it motivates us, changes us, and energizes us: it makes our eyes shine, puts a spring in our step, and focuses all our divided attentions into a single, laser-intense direction".[3] In regarding our hearts and minds, Jeremiah suggests,

> Having our hearts set on Christ means that our wills, our emotions, our hopes and dreams are centered on Him. The phrase set your mind means "to have understanding; to be wise; to feel, to think, to have an opinion, to judge; to direct one's mind to a thing; to seek or to strive for, to seek one's interests or advantage." In other words, it is the mental discipline of directed thinking.
>
> That's the positive command, but it is accompanied by a warning against the negative: "Seek those things which are above . . . not those things which are on the earth" (Col. 3:1-2). Immediately we find ourselves questioning that way of life. Paul isn't telling us to forego the physical challenges and chores of everyday life, while sitting and ruminating on heaven and angels. He is saying that our ultimate concern should be with heavenly realities and values, governed by the presence and power of Christ, who sits at the right hand of the Father . . . The Christian trains his mind to see those two alternatives, and to give precedence to the things of God.[4]

Where are we going and why am I in a handbasket?

Yet, throughout history, other individuals have found that, by conforming to God's moral standards, the Lord has blessed them with:

- wealth
- happiness
- spiritual health
- protection from enemies (human and otherwise)

It is possible that the problems our world faces today financially, morally, and religiously are the result of poor moral choices.

In the opening passage quoted in 2 Tim. We are warned that the following will be characteristic of people—they will be:

- lovers of themselves
- lovers of money
- boastful
- proud
- abusive
- disobedient to their parents
- ungrateful
- unholy
- without love
- unforgiving
- slanderous
- without self-control
- brutal
- not lovers of the good
- treacherous
- rash
- conceited
- lovers of pleasure rather than lovers of God
- having a form of godliness but denying its power

In his book, *Futurecast*, George Barna reports on the polls which reflect the moral condition of America. Startling statistics from his studies reveal:

- 25% of adults in the United States have never been married—many fear a failed marriage.
- Americans have become comfortable maintaining a belief in opposites—the importance of marriage and the acceptability of divorce.
- America has 3-4 times more cohabiting couples than couples getting married during a year.

- 41% of cohabiting couples have at least one child together—these children are three times more likely to have a child of their own out of wedlock and six times more likely to commit suicide.
- In 2008, 41% of all births were to unwed mothers—a new record.
- The number of births to women 35 and older has risen 64% in the past 20 years.
- In 1980, the book, *In Search of Excellence* was published. If studied today, the book would have to be called *Satisfied with Adequacy*, indicating a major shift in work ethic. p. 55
- We are losing a national sense of etiquette. Civility has gone the way of the dinosaur.
- World-view has shifted from a Christian God to a Shapeless God.
- Most adults no longer believe that absolute moral or spiritual truth exists—relativism is the rule of the day.
- Pop culture has shifted our attention from the marvelous deeds of true heroes to the vacuous words and absurd lifestyles of celebrities . . . A society built on its attentiveness to heroes will have heart and hope. A society devoted to celebrities will debase itself through an obsession with fame, frivolity, superficiality, and gossip.
- Our focus has shifted from knowledge to experience.
- 55%of born-again Christians leaned toward making abortion legal compared to 38% who would choose to make it illegal.
- Feelings-based morality is as common among born-again Christians as non-Christians. [5]

Barna cites a 2010 Gallup poll, as showing the following attitudes are morally acceptable:

- Divorce—69% say it is acceptable—up from 59% in 2001

- Gambling described as acceptable by 61%
- 59% believe that sexual intercourse between an unmarried man and woman is acceptable(up from 53% in 2001 and 2002)
- 54% claim that having a baby outside of marriage is acceptable—up from 45 % in 2002
- 52% see gay or lesbian relations are morally acceptable—up from 38% in 2002 [6]

Sexual Intimacy

Barna cites a 2010 Gallup poll as showing the following attitudes are morally acceptable:

> (Almost) everyone's doing it, an article in *Relevant* magazine, reports that a surprising new study shows Christians are having pre-marital sex and abortions as much (or more) than non-Christians. "Eighty percent of young, unmarried Christians have had sex. Two-thirds have been sexually active in the last year. Even though, according to a recent Gallup poll, 76% of evangelicals believe sex outside of marriage is morally wrong." [7]

Marriage

A Pew Research Center study of social and demographic trends published in November 2010 entitled, "The Decline of Marriage and Rise of New Families," reported on a number of significant changes in marriage patterns in American families:

- **The Class-Based Decline in Marriage**. About half (52%) of all adults in this country were married in 2008; back in 1960, seven-in-ten (72%) were. This decline has occurred along class lines. In 2008, there was a 16 percentage point gap in marriage rates between college graduates (64%) and those with a high school diploma or less (48%). In 1960, this gap had been just four percentage points (76% vs. 72%).

- **Is Marriage Becoming Obsolete?** Nearly four-in-ten survey respondents (39%) say that it is: In 1978 when *Time* magazine posed this question to registered voters, just 28% agreed. Those most likely to agree include those who are a part of the phenomenon (e.g. 62% of cohabiting parents) as well as those most likely to be troubled by it (e.g. 42% of self-described conservatives). Despite these growing uncertainties, Americans are more upbeat about the future of marriage and family (i.e. 67% say they are optimistic) than about the future of the country's educational system (50% optimistic), its economic system (46% optimistic) or its morals and ethics (41% optimistic).
- **An Ambivalent Public**. Seven-in-ten (69%) say the trend toward more single women having children is bad for society, and 61% say that a child needs both a mother and father to grow up happily.
- **Group Differences**. The young are more accepting than the old of the emerging arrangements; the secular are more accepting than the religious; liberals are more accepting than conservatives; the unmarried are more accepting than the married; and, in most cases, blacks are more accepting than whites. The net result of all these group differences is a nearly even three-way split among the full public. A third (34%) say, "the growing variety of family arrangements is a good thing; 29% say it is a bad thing and 32% say it makes little or no difference."
- **The Resilience of Families**. Three-quarters of all adults (76%) say their family is the most important element of their life; 75% say they are very satisfied with their family life, and more than eight-in-ten say the

family they live in now is as close as (45%) or closer than (40%) the family in which they grew up. However, on all of these questions, married adults give more positive responses than do unmarried adults.

- **The Definition of Family**. By emphatic margins, the public does not see marriage as the only path to family formation. Fully 86% say a single parent and child constitute a family; nearly as many (80%) say an unmarried couple living together with a child is a family; and 63% say a gay or lesbian couple raising a child is a family. The presence of children clearly matters in these definitions. If a cohabiting couple has no children, a majority of the public says they are not a family. Marriage matters, too. If a childless couple is married, 88% consider them to be a family.
- **The Ties that Bind.** In response to a question about which they would assist with money or caregiving in a time of need, Americans express a greater sense of obligation toward relatives—including relatives by way of fractured marriages—than toward best friends. The ranking of relatives aligns in a predictable hierarchy. More survey respondents express an obligation to help out a parent (i.e. 83% would feel very obligated) or grown child (77%) than say the same about a stepparent (55%) or a step or half sibling (43%). However, when asked about one's best friend, just 39% say they would feel a similar sense of obligation.
- **Changing Spousal Roles**. In the past 50 years, women have reached near parity with men as a share of the workforce and have begun to outpace men in educational attainment. About six-in-ten wives work today, nearly double the share in 1960. More than six-in-ten (62%) survey respondents endorse the modern marriage in which the husband and wife both work and

both take care of the household and children; this is up from 48% in 1977. Even so, the public hasn't entirely discarded the traditional male breadwinner template for marriage. Some 67% of survey respondents say that in order to be ready for marriage, it's very important for a man to be able to support his family financially; just 33% say the same about a woman.

- **The Impact on Children**. The share of births to unmarried women has risen dramatically over the past half century, from 5% in 1960 to 41% in 2008. There are notable differences by race: Among black women giving birth in 2008, 72% were unmarried. This compares with 53% of Hispanic women giving birth and 29% of white women. Overall, the share of children raised by a single parent is not as high as the share born to an unwed mother, but it too has risen sharply—to 25% in 2008, up from 9% in 1960. The public believes children of single parents face more challenges than other children—38% say, "A lot more challenges" and another 40% say, "a few more challenges."

  Survey respondents see even more challenges for children of gay and lesbian couples (51% say they face, "a lot more challenges.") and children of divorce (42% say they face, "a lot more challenges.").

- **In Marriage, Love Trumps Money**. Far more married adults say that love (93%), making a lifelong commitment (87%) and companionship (81%) are very important reasons to get married than say the same about having children (59%) or financial stability (31%). Unmarried adults order these items the same way. However, when asked if they agree that there is only one true love for every person, fewer than three-in-ten (28%) survey respondents say, I do.

- **Higher Marriage Rates in U.S. than in Europe.** 7.4% in U.S. vs. 4.9% in Europe were reported in a 2006 Pew Research study. [8]

Divorce

- By age 45, more than 33% of Americans born in the 1950s had divorced
- Divorce is common for many Americans.
- Among those whose marital histories are fairly complete, i.e., those born before 1950, 33% had divorced by age 45, and 40% by age 55.
- A 2006 Pew study reported that divorce is more prevalent in the U.S. than in the European Union: 3.7 divorces per 1000 people in the U.S. vs. 2.1 divorces per 1000 people in the EU. Some of this may result from a higher prevalence of cohabitation in the EU: 5.5% of over 20-year-old Americans vs. from 8.7-11.8% in Western Europe and lower rates (1.3-4.4%) in Southern and Eastern Europe). [9]

Cohabitation

Barna, quoting a U.S. Census Bureau, *Current Population Survey* in 2010, cites the following:

- One in 10 couples living together is unmarried
- Since 1960, the number of unmarried co-residential couples increased from slightly more than 1 percent (1.1%) of all couples to more than 10 percent (10.1%).[10]

One of the marked shifts in values is reflected in a 2002 report of the National Marriage Project authored by David Popenoe, Ph.D & Barbara Dafoe Whitehead, Ph.D.

The report states:

- "By 2000, the total number of unmarried couples in America was almost 4.75 million, up from less than half a million in 1960."
- "In 2000, 41% of all unmarried-couple households included a child under eighteen, up from only 21% in 1987." [11]

Clearly, moral values regarding physical intimacy have shifted to a place that would not be affirmed by an earlier generation or two and would not be recognized as conforming to the standards of the Bible.

Homosexuality

A Pew Research Center poll taken in October 2010 reported:

> More Americans continue to oppose gay marriage than support it, according to [a] poll, which was released October 2010 by the Pew Research Center. But for the first time since Pew starting asking about same sex marriage 15 years ago; fewer than half of those polled said they oppose legalizing the institution.
>
> - 42 percent of Americans favor same-sex marriage.
> - 48 percent oppose it.

In polls conducted in 2009:

- 37 percent favored same-sex marriage
- 54 percent were opposed

There were significant differences of opinions along age, racial and political party lines. On homosexual marriage, the new poll found:

- "Americans in the so-called Millennial Generation—those born after the 1980s—favor gay marriage by 53 percent to 39 percent, the poll found. Among those born between 1928 and 1945, just 29 percent favor allowing gays and lesbians to marry legally, while 59 percent are opposed."

- "Among Democrats, 53 percent support legalized gay marriage, while just 24 percent of Republicans do."
- "And while whites are evenly divided over gay marriage, the poll found, blacks oppose legalizing the institution by a wide margin." [12]

In 1993, U.S. Congress, in response to initiatives from the Lesbian, Gay, Bisexual, and Transgender (LGBT) lobby, enacted the Don't Ask, Don't Tell legislation prohibiting homosexual personnel from serving in the active-duty military. The policy protected individuals of those particular persuasions from harassment or abuse by straight military members and directed (LGBT) individuals from revealing their choice on pain of discharge from the military to enable maintaining the high standards of morale, good order and discipline amongst the troops.

In 2011 the act was repealed, removing the restriction, effective in September 2011, and allowing lesbian and gay personnel to serve. Behaviors contrary to the maintenance of good order and discipline are still prohibited by the *Uniform Code of Military Justice* (UCMJ). However, transgender and transsexual people may ***not*** serve in the military.

In April 2011, the four branches of the military began the necessary indoctrination training of service members prior to implementing the repeal.

Within the media (e.g. TV, motion pictures, etc.), it is a rare presentation that does not have a token homosexual portrayed today. TV series: (i.e. *Gray's Anatomy, Modern Family,* etc.) have a regular or occasional character living the lifestyle. Movies such as *Mrs. Doubtfire, Lincoln Lawyer, Four Weddings and a Funeral,* etc. likewise portray seemingly normal characters who live a homosexual lifestyle.

The education system also teaches tolerance for people who have adopted a homosexual lifestyle. Many liberal educators subtly or overtly denigrate anyone or any organization which fails to tolerate or encourage homosexual behavior.

There is very clear, marked movement away from Christian standards of the past to the *anything goes* standards of today. We are heading into the realization of the warning Paul gave to Timothy in his second epistle:

> In the last days . . . People will be lovers of themselves . . . disobedient to their parents . . . unholy . . . without self-control . . . not lovers of the good . . . lovers of pleasure rather than lovers of God—having a form of godliness but denying its power. (2 Tim. 3:2-5 NIV)

The Trendwatch website in a 2010 article entitled: *Casual Collapse*, described some random indicators of social and cultural change regarding homosexuality: [12]

- 38 countries now recognize same-sex marriages or civil partnerships, including South Africa and Argentina. (Source: Wikipedia).
- In August 2010, a Voice of India poll showed that almost a third of Indians in Bangalore and Mumbai support same-sex partnerships, a figure that would have been unheard of only a few years ago.
- Shanghai hosted mainland China's first Gay Pride event in June 2009.

British Prime Minister David Cameron has threatened to withhold UK aid from governments that do not reform legislation banning homosexuality:

> The UK prime minister said he raised the issue with some of the states involved at the Commonwealth Heads of Government Meeting in Perth, Australia . . . . Human rights reform in the Commonwealth was one issue that leaders failed to reach agreement on at the summit . . . . Mr. Cameron says

> those receiving UK aid should "adhere to proper human rights" . . . . Ending the bans on homosexuality was one of the recommendations of an internal report into the future relevance of the Commonwealth . . . . Mr. Cameron's threat applies only to one type of bilateral aid known as general budget support, and would not reduce the overall amount of aid to any one country . . . . Malawi has already had some of its budget support suspended over concerns about its attitude to gay rights. Concerns have also been raised with the governments of Uganda and Ghana. [14]

Scholastically

A critical literature review study of character education by Joseph Garland Whitley of the College of William and Mary in Williamsburg, Virginia mentions:

> All across the United States, teachers, administrators, parents, and other [vital] stakeholders are pondering the moral state of schools and the students that they are dedicated to educating. Many are witnessing what they believe is an erosion of morals and values among students and feel that this perceived lack of morals and values is contributing to:
>
> - low test scores
> - poor attendance
> - lack of discipline
> - general lack of respect for authority
>
> With this in mind, many teachers and administrators are now implementing programs in their schools to promote good morals and values that they feel are no longer being taught in the home. These character education programs seek to restore what many feel is the lack of moral education in the home. While many view character education as an integral and quite necessary component of education, many

> call this type of education into question. Some view these programs as completely ineffective, while others view them as a domain the schools should leave to the parents. [15]

This educator highlights problems experienced and reported by parents and educators and responds to efforts to reverse the decline in the moral education of America's youth. While cheating has been a problem for many children and youth for as long as schools have been in existence, today, technological advances have made it easier.

Cell phones, texting, iPods, smart phones, etc. are allowing students to cheat in many more ways than ever before. Back in the day, writing notes on one's hand or other body parts or surreptitiously looking at another student's work, when the teacher wasn't looking, were common methods used to cheat on tests. Competition for entrance into college, peer pressure, and the sheer (i.e. false) joy of passing a test to stay in school or out of trouble with parents, the principal, or law enforcement motivate students to cheat. Drugs common in the world of youth hamper the efforts of students to succeed and drive some to cheat to get by.

Schools and teachers have shown themselves to not be above cheating to qualify for continued receipt of funds to do their work and sustain programs important to their own or the school's prestige. With national standards such as *No Child Left Behind* (2001) creating stringent requirements for continued government support of education and employment for teachers and staff, the stress level is high enough to motivate people to lower their own standards and cheat or dissemble in response. Situational ethics have become increasingly important and many times reign supreme in decisions made by people who ought to know better and set better examples.

Internet

The Internet has enabled people to communicate all around the globe. Natives in jungle huts have access to the immense amount of information posted and streamed from its resources. While there is much good, there is also much evil available—from preaching the gospel to pornography. Where pornography was previously available in either print or visual formats, now inappropriate images, sound, and stories are proffered to anyone desiring to have their lusts fed with such material. Parents are encouraged to limit the web sites their children have access to. The seamier side of the Internet presents child porn, opportunities for sexual liaison, frank sexual images (e.g. both male and female), etc.

Internet regulators approved a new web suffix for adult entertainment in March 2011. First proposed in 2003, the *Internet Corporation for Assigned Names and Numbers* (ICANN) approved the controversial .xxx domain despite objections from the U.S. government, which threatened to override ICANN if necessary. Their somewhat flawed reasoning is that having a separate internet domain for adult entertainment:

> Will provide individuals and parents who wish to avoid adult entertainment sites the opportunity to filter out unwanted .xxx material. . . . The backers of the scheme said that it will provide reassurance to those visiting pornography websites that they are protected from the risk of viruses, identity theft, credit card fraud and inadvertent exposure to child abuse images. . . . [Surprisingly, the plan] drew criticism from some parts of the adult entertainment business, who said that forcing sex sites into a specific corner of the internet would inevitably increase censorship. [16]

An article published by *British Broadcasting Corporation* (BBC) *News* stated:

> Two of the internet's biggest pornography firms are suing the net's address regulator, ICANN, over its introduction of the .xxx suffix.
>
> Manwin Licensing and Digital Playground have also filed a lawsuit against ICM Registry [LLC], which is running the

> new top-level domain name (TLD) . . . . Much of the adult industry also opposed the idea, saying it would raise costs and could lead to a "ghettoisation" of the industry . . . . Manwin—which runs the Playboy websites—issued a press release alongside the lawsuit claiming that ICM was charging annual registration fees of about $60 per address. It claimed that was 10 times the fee charged for other comparable top-level domain names.
>
> It said costs mounted up because website owners had to register mis-spelt versions of their addresses to prevent cyber squatters exploiting them . . . . "The claims are baseless and without merit and will be defended vigorously," ICM Registry president Stuart Lawley said. [7]

Parental Rights

The rights of loving, non-abusive parents to raise their own children are being abrogated by the Federal Government and international guidelines published under the auspices of the *United Nations* (UN).

The UN Commission on the Rights of the Child has proposed guidelines for a child's rights that have been ratified by most nations, except the United States, and published as the *Convention on the Rights of the Child* (CRC or UNCRC).

In Article I, Section 2, Paragraph 2, the CRC says: "States Parties shall take all appropriate measures to ensure that the child is protected against all forms of discrimination or punishment on the basis of the status, activities, expressed opinions, or beliefs of the child's parents, legal guardians, or family members."[18]

This application of international law to American families has resulted in denying parents of their right to decide what is in the best interest of their children.

Article 5 of the CRC says: "States Parties shall respect the responsibilities, rights and duties of parents or, where applicable, the members of the extended family or community as provided for by local custom, legal guardians or other persons legally responsible for the child, to provide, in a manner consistent with the evolving capacities of the child, appropriate direction and guidance in the exercise by the child of the rights recognized in the present Convention." [19]

The *United Nations Children's Fund (*UNICEF) is the branch of the United Nations tasked with overseeing the CRF. The CRF:

> . . . [W]as adopted and opened for signature on November 20, 1989, by the United Nations General Assembly. After being ratified by the required 20 nations, it came into force on September 2, 1990. As of November 2009, 194 countries have ratified it. Out of the members of the United Nations, only Somalia and the United States of America have not ratified it.[20]

The Federal government of the United States, though not a signatory to the CRF, is choosing to adopt some of its principles and apply them to court decisions made in America. The ParentalRights.org web site reports on the shift in judicial policy in the Supreme Court of the United States as used in Troxel v. Granville, 530 U.S. 57 (2000). The shift is described as:

> The liberty interest at issue in this case—the interest of parents in the care, custody, and control of their children—is perhaps the oldest of the fundamental liberty interests recognized by this Court.
>
> In light of this extensive precedent, it cannot now be doubted that the Due Process Clause of the Fourteenth Amendment protects the fundamental right of parents to make decisions concerning the care, custody, and control of their children.

> Unfortunately, they vacated the earlier strict scrutiny test that required proof of harm before the government could interfere with parental rights, instead granting to judges the power to balance parental rights on a case-by-case basis.
>
> If a parent's decision of the kind at issue here becomes subject to judicial review, the court must accord at least some special weight to the parent's own determination. We would be hesitant to hold that specific non-parental visitation statutes violate Parental rights are being eroded to the moral detriment of our nation. [21]

In summary

Christian philosopher and theologian John Piper writes:

> Our final summary emphasis should be this: In 1 Timothy 6, Paul's purpose is to help us lay hold on eternal life and not lose it. Paul never dabbles in unessentials [sp]. He lives on the brink of eternity. That's why he sees things so clearly. He stands there like God's gatekeeper and treats us like reasonable Christian Hedonists: you want life which is life indeed; don't you (verse 19)? You don't want ruin, destruction and pangs of heart, do you (verses 9-10)? You do want all the gain that godliness can bring; don't you (verse 6)? Then use the currency of Christian Hedonism wisely: do not desire to be rich, be content with the wartime necessities of life, set your hope fully on God, guard yourself from pride and let your joy in God overflow in a wealth of liberality to a lost and needy world.[22]

But God . . . !

CHAPTER 6

Ethical Decline

[1] But mark this: There will be terrible times in the last days. [2] People will be lovers of themselves, lovers of money, boastful, proud, abusive, disobedient to their parents, ungrateful, unholy, [3] without love, unforgiving, slanderous, without self-control, brutal, not lovers of the good, [4] treacherous, rash, conceited, lovers of pleasure rather than lovers of God— [5] having a form of godliness but denying its power. Have nothing to do with them. (2 Tim. 3:1-5 NIV)

As forecasted in scripture, the last days will see a decline in ethics throughout the world.

To be ethical has to do with conformity to behavioral standards set by the society in which the standards are established. The *Collins English Dictionary* defines *ethics* as: [1]

- The philosophical study of the moral value of human conduct and the rules and principles that ought to govern it; moral philosophy.
- A social, religious, or civil code of behavior considered correct, esp. That of a particular group, profession, or individual.
- The moral fitness of a decision, course of action, etc.: he doubted the ethics of their verdict.

Will Durant, in *Our Oriental Heritage*, (previously quoted in Chapter 5) provides insight into the moral development of societal cultures which also applies to a culture's ethical development. (1963)

Two kinds of standards set limits on a person's moral or ethical conduct: mankind's and God's. Man's standards, embodied in human society and flawed, as a result of failing to obey God, provide guidelines for behavior derive from a sometimes warped manner of reasoning. God's standards derive from His perfect plan for mankind.

Over three millennia ago, God set standards for our work and personal relationships and had them recorded in scripture. These seem somewhat rarely followed in the world today:

- Love God above all (Deut. 6:5).
- Love your neighbor as yourself (Lev. 19:18).
- Treat others as you want to be treated (Matt. 7:12).

Since the historical event commonly known as "The Fall" recounted in Genesis 3, mankind has strayed from the Creator's plans. Like moral standards, the ethical standards of many societies have born little resemblance to biblical standards. Those societies remained weak, divisive, and poor. Disease, famine, internal discord, attacks from enemies, immorality and depravity of all sorts have marked those societies as they attempted to live life their own way in contravention to God's way. The Apostle Paul warned Timothy about such things taking place in the last days. (2 Tim. 3:1-9)

Yet, throughout history, other individuals have found that, by conforming to God's standards, the Lord has blessed them with wealth, happiness, spiritual health, and protection from enemies (e.g. human and otherwise). It is possible that the problems our world faces today financially, ethically, and religiously are the result of poor choices.

It is true that ethically and morally ignorant people have ignored God's standards and become poorer for it. In the mid-twentieth century, certain ethical standards were commonly accepted in America:

- Don't lie.
- Don't cheat your customers.
- Give honest value in your products and services.

While there have been *snake-oil* salesmen and charlatans throughout the past two or more centuries, society did not readily accept their behaviors. Today, if one can do things not commonly accepted by society and get away with it that is ok. After all, *everyone wants to get theirs!*

Massive schemes such as the one perpetrated by Bernard (i.e. Bernie) Madoff are bleeding the heart of America. In one of the greatest financial scandals of our time, Madoff perpetrated a *Ponzi* scheme that defrauded thousands of investors and drained the retirement accounts of many individual and corporate investors.

Charitable foundations which invested with funds managed by Madoff lost billions of dollars. His scheme required a flow of new cash to pay off investors who were lured by the promise of 10-12% returns on their investments.

Where are we going and why am I in a handbasket?

The lust for financial gain drew many to trust Madoff's expertise in investing and later become betrayed for it. Financial investment advisors, who should have known better, fell for the scheme and recommended to their customers that they invest as well.

The *Wall Street Journal* reported on Madoff's conviction and sentencing:

> Bernard Madoff, the self-confessed author of the biggest financial swindle in history, was sentenced to the maximum 150 years behind bars for what his judge called, "An extraordinarily evil" fraud that shook the nation's faith in its financial and legal systems and took "a staggering toll" on rich and poor alike. [2]

The Better Business Bureau often warns, "If it seems too good to be true, it probably is"!

A somewhat common event for some political candidates is typified in the situation for Kansas Secretary of State Kris Kobach's campaign, reported in the *Kansas City Star* on October 26, 2011. The campaign:

> Was fined $5,000 Wednesday for mistakes made in filing expense and contribution reports for the 2010 election . . . The Governmental Ethics Commission voted 7-2 to impose the maximum fine after questioning Kobach's campaign treasurer, state Rep. Tom Arpke of Salina. At issue was nearly $80,000 that was omitted from the reports . . . Commission Chairwoman Sabrina Standifer said the maximum fine was imposed, in part, because the campaign maintained that it reported the omissions to ethics officials. [3]

Ethical Shifts

A 2010 article on the Trendwatch website discusses the demise of beliefs and rituals that describe a shift in the ethical values of consumers in American society:

> In mature consumer economies, a *casual collapse* seems unstoppable: we're talking the ongoing demise of many

> beliefs, rituals, formal requirements and laws that modern societies have held dear, which continue to 'collapse' without causing the apocalyptic aftermath often predicted . . . Our mature consumers have grown up completely immersed in consumer culture—they *get* the deal. But as savvy, streetwise consumers, they are bored, if not downright distrustful of the conventional consumer-producer relationship, and now look for brands and products that are more authentic, more human, and quite simply more mature. [4]

World Corruption Increasing

The level of global corruption is indicative of the decline in ethics in societies around the world.

Annually, *Transparency International* (TI) publishes a Corruption Index Report. TI:

> Is [a] global civil society organization leading the fight against corruption. Through more than 90 chapters worldwide and an international secretariat in Berlin, TI raises awareness of the damaging effects of corruption and works with partners in government, business and civil society to develop and implement effective measures to tackle it.

Their 2010 index shows the highest corruption takes place in developing countries, but is known to some extent in all countries:

> With governments committing huge sums to tackle the world's most pressing problems, from the instability of financial markets to climate change and poverty, corruption remains an obstacle to achieving much needed progress. The 2010 *Corruption Perceptions Index* (CPI) shows that nearly three quarters of the 178 countries in the index score below five, on a scale from 10 (i.e. very clean) to 0 (i.e. highly corrupt). These results indicate a serious corruption problem . . . Denmark, New Zealand and Singapore are tied

> at the top of the list with a score of 9.3, followed closely by Finland and Sweden at 9.2. At the bottom is Somalia with a score of 1.1, slightly trailing Myanmar and Afghanistan at 1.4 and Iraq at 1.5. Notable among decliners over the past year are some of the countries most affected by a financial crisis precipitated by transparency and integrity deficits. Among those improving in the past year, the general absence of the *Organization for Economic Co-operation and Development* (OECD) states underlines the fact that all nations need to bolster their good governance mechanisms . . . . The message is clear: across the globe, transparency and accountability are critical to restoring trust and turning back the tide of corruption. Without them, global policy solutions to many global crises are at risk. [5]
>
> [n.b. OECD states include 34 countries partnering as an international economic organization to stimulate economic progress and world trade.]

OECD is an international economic organization of 34 countries founded in 1961. It is a forum of countries committed to democracy and the market economy, providing a platform to compare policy experiences, seek answers to common problems, identify good practices, and co-ordinate domestic and international policies of its members.

OECD Initiatives

While OECD initiatives such as the Integrity Framework are a step in the right direction, there is much more to be done. The Integrity Framework includes:

> The OECD good governance approach helps countries map out sources of and incentives for corruption. It also develops measures to promote a culture of integrity, transparency and accountability . . . The OECD vision of fostering integrity in public service is expressed through the Integrity

> Framework which combines integrity instruments, processes, structures, conditions for the implementation and dynamic development in public organizations . . . . The OECD helps countries prevent conflict of interest and corruption in public service. It focuses on vulnerable areas such as public procurement and contract management, lobbying and political-administrative interface . . . . Based on review and analysis of good country practices, the OECD developed a series of policy instruments, implementation guidelines and practical tools to help policy makers and managers promote integrity and foster resistance to corruption in the public sector.
>
> Integrity is the corner stone of good governance. Fostering integrity and preventing corruption in the public sector support a level playing field for businesses and is essential to maintaining trust in government . . . . 'Integrity' refers to the application of values, principles and norms in the daily operations of public sector organizations. Governments are under growing pressure from the public to use information, resources and authority for intended purposes. [6]

Governments and organizations must be willing to adopt such initiatives. But is it likely to happen? One does not want to be overly pessimistic, but scripture seems to indicate that it is not likely to be seen until Jesus returns.

Christians believe that it will take a genuine move of the Holy Spirit to turn the situation around. Only a true world-wide revival can reverse the current trends. While this is true, prophesy indicates that it may not become so.

The result of the level of corruption is that enterprises have risen and are available to profitably address the problem. One such company, describing themselves as *ethical engineers*, is Vogelwede & Associates, advertising themselves as Corruption Control Consultants. They take a multi-level approach to diagnosis and correction of the identified corruption.

They have identified the different types of corruption in business and government: [7]

Favoritism

- supply chain
- distribution
- nepotism
- discrimination
- prejudice

Authority

- privilege
- abuse
- contract
- embezzlement
- harassment

Tribute

- commissions
- tapping
- bribes (e.g. *mordida* or *baksheesh*)
- extortion
- protection

Competence

- indolence
- ineptitude
- resistance
- cheating
- theft

Note that the causes of corruption listed below all derive from the list in 2 Tim. 3:1-9:

Need

- personal gain

Opportunity

- deficient internal controls

Rationalization

- not a punishable infraction

Tolerance

- peer group acceptance

Corruption tends to evolve from one stage to another:

Spontaneous → Colluded → Compromised → Organized → Franchised

Thus it begins with one unethical individual and evolves until it becomes endemic in the culture (business or government). Corruption in its basic form is sin and has an impact in many aspects of an enterprise:

- higher costs
- squandered resources
- ruined lives
- stalled development
- lower quality
- closed business
- derelict governments
- perpetual poverty

A 2002 article published online by Wharton School of Business under their Knowledge@Wharton banner on Business Ethics highlights the problem of bribery for the business world:

There's no doubt that corruption, endemic in emerging economies around the world, throws economic development into chaos. It affects decisions made by bureaucrats, degrades the quality of those in power, and discourages foreign investment. It's also an increasingly hot business topic, with a growing number of influential business and political leaders from around the globe regularly pinpointing corruption as one of the greatest threats to global economic development . . . "Corruption and bribery have moved to the forefront in discussions about business," says Wharton legal studies Professor Philip M. Nichols. "The list of countries that have been politically or economically crippled by corruption continues to grow, and businesses with long-term interests abroad will ultimately be harmed by any plans that include bribery" . . . . Bribery, of course, is the most widespread form of corruption, and corporate strategies for dealing with bribe requests vary. According to Nichols, some companies opt to pay, sometimes damaging their public images and making it more difficult to refuse future requests. Others have the sheer bulk and revenues to successfully and consistently say "no." Oil giant Texaco, for example, has such a formidable reputation for refusing to pay bribes that its jeeps are often waved through even remote African border crossings without paying a penny . . . A key, Nichols suggests, is wiring this no-bribe ideal into a corporation's culture, starting with a corporate code for managers and employees, affiliates and potential business partners. But coming to grips with what appears to be an international groundswell of corruption is far from a simple matter. Nichols believes that unraveling and explaining the mechanics of corruption is critical to helping the growing body of government and corporate organizations trying to fight it. [8]

Grand Schemes

The *Economist* reported in an October 29, 2011 article about the World Bank "blast[ing] registration for corrupt ends." Companies incorporated in prominent countries have been found to conceal their real ownership and bank accounts. The article cited 150 cases involving 817 companies in corruption cases. The countries involved include (e.g. in order of worst corruption): United States, Switzerland, Britain, Bahamas, Nigeria, Cyprus, Hong Kong, Antigua and Barbuda, Jersey, and Lichtenstein. [9]

Contemporary novels, movies, and TV dramas often depict organizations (criminal enterprises, and other companies) which have "off-shore" accounts that resist investigation by authorities. These schemes have become part of the modern global culture even though most companies and organizations do not indulge in such practices and do maintain some level of ethical integrity.

All power tends to corrupt

The old adage, *power corrupts but absolute power corrupts absolutely*, has been tested by three social scientists and found to be somewhat misleading. Nathanael Fast of the University of Southern California, Nir Halevy of Stanford University, and Adam Galinsky of Northwestern University collaborated in a study to test the classic *little Hitler combination of low status and high power.* They observed that lots of psychological experiments have been done on the effects of status and lots on the effects of power. But few, if any, have been done on both combined. The study proved that:

> Participants who had both status and power did not greatly demean their partners. They chose an average of 0.67 demeaning activities for those partners to perform. Low-power/low-status and low-power/high-status participants behaved similarly. They chose, on average, 0.67 and 0.85 demeaning activities. However, participants who were

> low in status but high in power—the classic *little Hitler* combination—chose an average of 1.12 deeply demeaning tasks for their partners to engage in. That was a highly statistically significant distinction. [10]

Example of power corruption

As reported by *NewsMax*.com:

> "The Egyptian military has been using a banned chemical agent [CR gas] to deal with hundreds of thousands of protesters, according to several news sources. At least 23 Egyptians have died and more than 1,700 have succumbed to a lethal gas military forces have been using during the past three days in clashes in and around Cairo's Tahrir Square.
>
> CR gas is an intense and lethal version of CS gas, called "tear gas," widely used by police for crowd control.
>
> Wikipedia notes that CR gas has effects that are "are approximately 6 to 10 times more powerful than those of CS gas." CR causes intense skin pain and irritation, and can lead to blindness and death by asphyxiation." [11]

Since the first protests in January 2011 over the oppressive regime of Hosni Mubarak began and then subsided with his abdication and subsequently his terminal illness and death, Egypt has experienced internal strife with attendant difficulty restraining or containing possible violence.

News Media

In recent years, the news media have moved from journalism to sensationalism. The liberal media have published in their many venues (e.g. print, TV, online video, and Internet) the message of the liberal politicians, while minimalizing the message of the conservative or moderate politicians. Some of this has gone on for many decades, but never before with the intensity it is today. The last major malfeasance by the liberal media was in the 1960s, when they reported on the Vietnam War protests.

In a commentary on the GOPUSA web site, Cliff Kincaid castigated Brian Williams of *NBC Nightly News* for his "going public with sensational and wild allegations against the police" for using pepper spray to subdue the protestors as he reported on the Occupy protest on the University of California-Davis (UC-Davis) campus.

According to Kincaid, Williams failed to do due diligence and report that many of those protesting on the UC-Davis campus were not even students, but rather radicals who had come on to campus to join and radicalize the protest.

Kincaid, Director of the AIM Center for Investigative Journalism, opined:

> "Clearly, Brian Williams of *NBC News* misled his viewers about what these *kids* really did. They flouted the law, interfering with the rights of others . . . It is time to examine who and what is behind the "Occupy" movement and why billionaire George Soros is financing it." [12]

This is illustrative of the loss of ethical reporting by the media. Many times, vital issues are ignored in favor of reporting on the more spectacular issues which sell ads. Profit or power motives seem to dominate decisions about priorities in reporting.

Ethical Abdication of American Politicians

So-called leaders in the United States government are abdicating their responsibility to uphold their oath of office. Senators swear (or affirm) the following:

> I do solemnly swear (or affirm) that I will support and defend the Constitution of the United States against all enemies, foreign and domestic; that I will bear true faith and allegiance to the same; that I take this obligation freely,

> without any mental reservation or purpose of evasion; and that I will well and faithfully discharge the duties of the office on which I am about to enter: So help me God.[13]

Members of the House of Representatives swear (or affirm) the following:

> I, do solemnly swear (or affirm) that I will support and defend the Constitution of the United States against all enemies, foreign and domestic; that I will bear true faith and allegiance to the same; that I take this obligation freely, without any mental reservation or purpose of evasion; and that I will well and faithfully discharge the duties of the office on which I am about to enter. So help me God.[14]

Note that both houses, swear (or affirm) that [they], "will support and defend the Constitution of the United States against all enemies, foreign and domestic." For these same individuals to abrogate this solemn responsibility to "support and defend" this nation by allowing international laws to override our Constitutional law is to clearly fail in their ethical responsibility to the American people.

Not only have politicians at the federal level relinquished their responsibility to *support and defend*: in the case of children as discussed in Chapter 5, but they are also failing to shoulder their responsibilities in the protection of rights granted by our Constitution.

American politicians are setting things up to force a disarming of the nation and abrogation of constitutional 2nd Amendment rights to bear arms. They do this by failing to veto *United Nations* (UN) gun control initiatives. ParentalRights.org reports on UN initiatives related to the UN Convention on the Rights of the Child signed by most, but not all UN member nations:

> The vast majority of Americans, regardless of their opinions on the increasing scope of international law, agree with the proposition that children should not be used as soldiers.

> Accordingly, much of the UN literature that addresses children and guns deals with this military-related issue.
>
> However, a second theme is quickly found in virtually all UN pronouncements about child soldiers and weapons. UN child's rights advocates believe, teach, and promote the idea that all private gun-ownership is dangerous for children, and that children have the right to grow up in a community that is free from all guns.[15]

The Obama presidency has been involved with a number of ethical violations, chief among which is the awarding of money ostensibly to jump-start green businesses and improve the employment during the current economic downturn. *Fox News*, ABC's *Good Morning America*, *Fox News Daily Caller* blog, and the *Washington Post* have all reported on Obama's pushing for money to support Solyndra, a solar cell company in which there are personal ties to Michelle Obama alleged.[16] [17] [18] [19]

While current laws do not prohibit congressmen from profiting from *insider trading*, the average American would be prosecuted for the same action. Jonathan Macey reported in the *Wall Street Journal* on the new initiative being proposed by Congress to limit the ability of legislators to buy stock on insider information. Macey noted:

> Members of Congress already get better health insurance and retirement benefits than other Americans. They are about to get better insider trading laws as well.
>
> Several academic studies show that the investment portfolios of congressmen and senators consistently outperform stock indices like the Dow and the S&P 500, as well as the portfolios of virtually all professional investors. Congressmen do better to an extent that is statistically significant, according to studies including a 2004 article about "abnormal" Senate returns by Alan J. Ziobrowski,

> Ping Cheng, James W. Boyd and Brigitte J. Ziobrowski in the Journal of Financial and Qualitative Analysis . . .
>
> Democrats' portfolios outperform the market by a whopping 9%. Republicans do well, though not quite as well. And the trading is widespread, although a higher percentage of senators than representatives trade—which is not surprising because senators outperform the market by an astonishing 12% on an annual basis.
>
> These results are not due to luck or the financial acumen of elected officials. They can be explained only by insider trading based on the nonpublic information that politicians obtain in the course of their official duties.
>
> Strangely, while insider trading by corporate insiders has long been the white collar crime equivalent of a major felony, *the Securities and Exchange Commission has determined that insider trading laws do not apply to members of Congress or their staff.* That is because, according to the SEC at least, these public officials do not owe the same legal duty of confidentiality that makes insider trading illegal by nonpoliticians.[20]

Low public approval ratings seems to be driving congress to at least attempt to appear as if they want to represent their constituencies ethically. They are introducing legislation to deny lawmakers the assumed right to engage in insider trading.

Larry Margasak, reporting in the *Huffington Post* in November 2011 said:

> Members of Congress, battling single digit approval ratings, are paying attention to the perception that some lawmakers enriched themselves through insider trading.
>
> Bills in the House and Senate are getting hearings, and the House Ethics Committee has sent out a memo

> reminding lawmakers that insider trading could violate the law and House rules.[21]

The *Chicago Tribune* in an opinion editorial, suggested:

> Congress members need to abide by the power of free markets and laws on insider trading.
>
> Everyone knows Congress has its share of wheeler-dealers, but stock traders? Yes, maybe more than we thought. Media reports have raised questions about whether elected representatives, along with their families and staffs, wring trading profits from information gleaned in backroom sessions on Capitol Hill.
>
> A recent "60 Minutes" segment highlighted the trading activity of Republican House Speaker John Boehner, of Ohio, Democratic Minority Leader Nancy Pelosi, of California, and Rep. Spencer Bachus, R-Ala., chairman of the House financial services committee.[22]

Former Presidential candidate, Governor Rick Perry of Texas, picked up on the editorial and was reported in *Politico* to have said in a *RedState* article:

> While the professional political punditry class is more interested in superfluous items like the political horse race and candidate attire, the reality is that members of both parties in Washington, D.C., are abusing their positions and ordinary Americans have had enough," the Texas governor writes, expressing his outrage at the recent allegations of congressional insider trading . . . "It's time to uproot and overhaul Washington," Perry wrote. "We can start with ensuring insider trading by members of Congress results in prison time, and not unseemly profits.[23]

A *CNN Money* report asked:

> How common is insider trading on the Hill? There is evidence to suggest that at least some past members of Congress beat the market with astonishing regularity.
>
> A 2004 academic study based on trades by senators from 1993 to 1998 found that taken together, the senators' portfolios beat the market by a whopping 12% per year.
>
> A follow-up study by the same authors on transactions made by roughly 300 House members between 1985 and 2001 found that a portfolio mimicking these purchases beat the market by about 6% annually.
>
> A study released earlier this year by researchers from Yale and the *Massachusetts Institute of Technology* (MIT) found that the average investor in Congress between 2004 and 2008 actually under-performed against the market by 2-3% annually.
>
> Whether this is the case with the current Congress isn't clear. A study released earlier this year by researchers from Yale and MIT found that the average investor in Congress between 2004 and 2008 actually under-performed against the market by 2-3% annually.[24]

Does this mean that the current congress is more ethical than previous ones or simply that the cockroaches are hiding until the lights go out?

Georgia State University professor Alan Ziobrowski, coauthor of the study the aforementioned study of Senate and House members, has cautiously opined, "I think what you're seeing is more or less a behavioral change. Whether or not it's permanent is rather doubtful . . . I think it's still quite possible to pick up information that no one else has access to." [25]

Ziobrowski summed up the problem well: "This is an issue of ethics, and it's an issue of people having faith in government," . . . "It's crucial that people believe that a congressman is not voting for his portfolio, but instead is voting for the benefit of his constituents."[26]

Boldness

In summary, as predicted by the Corruption Consulting model, ethics is becoming a foreign concept to people throughout the world. Perpetrators of evil schemes are becoming bolder in their deception and plans. And, at the same time, it seems that victims are becoming less discerning in their resistance to the schemes. What ever happened to *Caveat Emptor* (Let the buyer beware)? Are we trusting government oversight too much?

Final thoughts . . .

Christians are exhorted to avoid living like the unbelievers do in their futile thinking but rather to be made new in matters of thinking (Eph. 4:17, 23; Rom. 12:1-2). Believers must place their trust solely in God and not yield to the temptations of the world's flawed values system.

But God . . . !

PART 3

POLITICS

- Subduing Israel has been the goal of many nations of the world over the centuries. It has only been the hand of God, which allows Israel to exist.
- The concept of world peace is being tested severely in the Middle East. Decades of attempts to achieve it has failed.
- A frightened world population, having seen the failure of traditional governments to solve global problems, is increasingly calling for a global governance solution.

CHAPTER 7

Attacks against Israel

5 "Announce in Judah and proclaim in
Jerusalem and say: 'Sound the trumpet
throughout the land!' Cry aloud and say:
'Gather together! Let us flee to the fortified
cities!' 6 Raise the signal to go to Zion! Flee for
safety without delay! For I am bringing disaster
from the north, even terrible destruction." 7 A
lion has come out of his lair; a destroyer of
nations has set out. He has left his place to lay
waste your land. Your towns will lie in ruins
without inhabitant. 8 So put on sackcloth,
lament and wail, for the fierce anger of the
LORD has not turned away from us. 9 "In that
day," declares the LORD, "the king and the
officials will lose heart, the priests will be
horrified, and the prophets will be appalled."
(Jer. 4:5-9 NIV)

From ancient times, the Promised Land was attacked by Israel's enemies. Some of the major enemies include:

- Amalekites—were a constant thorn in the side of the Israelites, until King David's troops defeated them. They opposed the movement of Moses and the Israelites, as they left Egypt and attempted to return to the land of Canaan.
- Philistines—Goliath, et al.
- Assyria—Sennacherib—scattered the northern ten tribes.
- Babylon—Nebuchadnezzar—Solomon's Temple destroyed—carried off the two southern tribes to 70 years of captivity.
- Rome—Titus in 70 A.D.—Herod's Temple destroyed.

Since the inception of Israel as a modern nation in 1948, Israel has been the object of attacks from her enemies:

- 1948—Arab coalition nations attacked
- 1956—Suez Canal Conflict
- 1967—Six-day War
- 1973—Yom Kippur attacks
- 1982—War with Lebanon & Hezbollah, augmented by 1500 Iranian Revolutionary Guard troops
- 1987-1993—First Palestinian Intifada
- 1991—Scud missile attacks from Iraq
- 2001-2009, 2011—Missile attacks from Gaza & Ramallah by Palestinians

Sometime in the future, a Russian (i.e. Magog) coalition led by Gog will attack Israel.

- ????—War of Gog & Magog. (Ezek.38:18)

God pronounced blessings for obedience and curses for disobedience for the nation of Israel. The ten northern tribes experienced curses for disobedience through the Assyrians by being scattered after they chose to follow the evil practices of Jeroboam. The two remaining tribes experienced God's anger and the resultant loss of Solomon's Temple—destroyed by Nebuchadnezzar, after they failed to obey God's instructions and were subsequently taken to Babylon for seventy years of captivity.

When Israel did obey God and sought His assistance to counter enemies coming against them, God was always true to His word and provided a way out of the difficulty for Israel. Some prominent examples include:

Moses and Joshua fighting the Amalekites. As long a Moses kept his hands raised in praise to God, Joshua prevailed in the battle. When Moses' arms became too tired to stay up, Aaron and Hur stood beside him to assist (Exod. 17:8-13).

Jehoshaphat was attacked by the armies of Amon, Moab, and Mt. Seir. The people of Amon, Moab and Mt. Seir decided that they would gang up on Judah and Jerusalem. All of the coalition came from the region we know today as Jordan. Mt. Seir was populated by a people called the Meunites, an Arab people who lived in the area near Petra and Bosrah (2 Chron. 20:1-26).

When Jehoshaphat learned from his sentinels in En Gedi of the imminent attack, he:

- Became alarmed.
- Resolved to inquire of the LORD.
- Proclaimed a fast for all Judah and people came from every village and sought the Lord.
- Prayed in the Temple, reminding God of His promises:

  "O LORD, God of our fathers, are you not the God who is in heaven? You rule over all the kingdoms of the nations. Power and might are in your hand, and

> no one can withstand you. O our God, did you not drive out the inhabitants of this land before your people Israel and give it forever to the descendants of Abraham your friend? They have lived in it and have built in it a sanctuary for your Name, saying, 'If calamity comes upon us, whether the sword of judgment, or plague or famine, we will stand in your presence before this temple that bears your Name and will cry out to you in our distress, and you will hear us and save us.' "But now here are men from Ammon, Moab and Mount Seir, whose territory you would not allow Israel to invade when they came from Egypt; so they turned away from them and did not destroy them (2 Chron. 20:6-10 NIV).

- Acknowledged that, "We do not know what to do, but our eyes are upon you."

After the people humbly prayed, God gave Jehoshaphat a plan through the prophet Jahaziel (2 Chron. 20:15-21 NIV):

- Jahaziel reminded him, "The battle is not yours, but God's."
- Tomorrow march down against them.
- You will not have to fight this battle.
- Take up your positions.
- Stand firm and see the deliverance the LORD will give you.
- Do not be afraid; do not be discouraged.
- Go out to face them tomorrow, and the LORD will be with you.
- Jehoshaphat appointed men to sing to the LORD and to praise him for the splendor of his holiness as they went out at the head of the army, saying: "Give thanks to the LORD, for his love endures forever."

God's plans always succeed and did in this case (2 Chron. 20:22-26 NIV):

- As they began to sing and praise, the LORD set ambushes against the men of Ammon and Moab and Mount Seir who were invading Judah, and they attacked and defeated one another. The three armies of the coalition fought amongst themselves—the men of Ammon and Moab rose up against the men from Mount Seir to destroy and annihilate them. After they finished slaughtering the men from Seir, they helped to destroy one another.
- The men of Judah only had to recover the plunder from the battle over the next three days.
- On the fourth day the men of Judah assembled in the Valley of Beracah, where they praised the LORD.

Hezekiah and Sennacherib—Hezekiah:

> . . . [T]ore his clothes and put on sackcloth and went into the temple of the LORD . . . . And Hezekiah prayed to the LORD: "O LORD, God of Israel, enthroned between the cherubim, you alone are God over all the kingdoms of the earth. You have made heaven and earth. Give ear, O LORD, and hear; open your eyes, O LORD, and see; listen to the words Sennacherib has sent to insult the living God. "It is true, O LORD, that the Assyrian kings have laid waste these nations and their lands. They have thrown their gods into the fire and destroyed them, for they were not gods but only wood and stone, fashioned by men's hands. Now, O LORD our God, deliver us from his hand, so that all kingdoms on earth may know that you alone, O LORD, are God." Then Isaiah son of Amoz sent a message to Hezekiah: "This is what the LORD, the God of Israel, says: I have heard your prayer concerning Sennacherib king of Assyria (2 Kings 19:1, 15-20 NIV).

Note Hezekiah's heart in this passage. He:

- Tore his clothes.
- Put on sackcloth.
- Went into the temple of the Lord.
- Prayed and sought the Lord.

All of this demonstrates an attitude of humble submission to God that pleases God. The result of Hezekiah's entreaty is recorded in 2 Kings 19:32-37, The Lord promised that Sennacherib would:

- not enter Jerusalem or shoot an arrow there
- not come before the city with a shield or build a siege ramp against it
- turn around and go home to Nineveh in Assyria

God promised to save the city for His and [King] David's sake. Then an angel put to death 185,000 men in the Assyrian camp overnight and Sennacherib returned to Nineveh, and then was killed by his sons in the temple of Nisroch, Sennacherib's god.

Later, when Hezekiah was *sick unto death*, he prayed a heart-felt prayer and asked the Lord to heal him. God heard Hezekiah and gave him a choice how he wanted to know for sure that the Lord was going to heal him and extend his life by fifteen years. Hezekiah chose for the sun to reverse course and its shadow to return up the stairway of Ahaz.

When deeply-felt and humble requests are made in accordance with God's will, He answers.

One might ask . . .

History provides a lens through which we can view the future. Although the investing mantra, *Past performance is no guarantee of future returns,* seems to indicate otherwise, being obedient to God will always produce the best results. As Moses, Jehoshaphat, Hezekiah, David, Paul,

Matthew, Luke, and John discovered, it is always appropriate to adhere to the Lord's guidance and achieve success.

John recorded in his little letter that when we follow God's plan, we are assured of His hearing us and granting what it is we need: "This is the confidence we have in approaching God: that if we ask anything according to his will, he hears us. And if we know that he hears us—whatever we ask—we know that we have what we asked of him" (1 John 5:14-15 NIV).

God told Solomon, one granted unusual wisdom by God for ruling His people, that when faced with extreme circumstances, "If my people, who are called by my name, will humble themselves and pray and seek my face and turn from their wicked ways, then will I hear from heaven and will forgive their sin and will heal their land" (2 Chron. 7:14 NIV).

Note that there are several parts to the promise—if God's people, called by His name, will:

- humble themselves
- pray and seek God's face
- turn from their wicked ways

Then, God will:

- hear from heaven
- forgive their sin
- heal their land

Each time in the long history of Israel that the people and their leaders followed God's guidance; He was found faithful to fulfill His promises. At times it seemed to take a while, but God always completes His plans and fulfills His promises. So, no matter how many enemies scheme, conspire or plot to annihilate the Jews or deny them what God has promised, His people will always prevail.

The problem of Israel's enemies . . .

The *under the radar problem* for those who actively or inadvertently become Israel's enemy's lies in God's recorded blessing to Abraham: "I will bless those who bless you, and whoever curses you I will curse . . ." (Gen. 12:3 NIV).

From the tenth through the sixteenth century, Jews in Europe experienced edicts of expulsion from over one dozen countries for various reasons. Two of the most prominent nations expelling Jews were England (1290) and Spain (1492). In fact, the British 1290 Edict of Expulsion has never been reversed. Both nations have born the pain of the curse of God economically for their treatment of Jews.

There is a supernatural curse attached to the land of Israel. It is a divine curse from God Himself to men and nations who, with malice aforethought (i.e. premeditative with malice), do harm to the Jewish people or attack the State of Israel.

Obadiah prophesied to Edom: "The day of the LORD is near for all nations. As you have done, it will be done to you; your deeds will return upon your own head" (Obad. 1:15). While written specifically to Edom, this applies to any nation that comes against Israel.

Zechariah wrote, "For this is what the LORD Almighty says:

> After he has honored me and has sent me against the nations that have plundered you—for whoever touches you touches the apple of his eye—I will surely raise my hand against them so that their slaves will plunder them. Then you will know that the LORD Almighty has sent me" (Zech. 2:8-9 NIV).

Zechariah is focusing on the near return of the restored Jewish community from Babylon while God is preparing to avenge His people by destroying their enemies.

There is clearly a price to be paid for being Israel's enemy.

In 1290, King Edward I issued an edict expelling all Jews from England. In 1492, King Ferdinand and Queen Isabella expelled all Jews from Spain. John Hagee wrote:

> In 1947, Great Britain voted against the Jewish people having a homeland in Palestine. Currently, England is charging members of the Israeli government as war criminals for their role in defending Israel from the rocket attacks of Hamas . . . Today, England is flooded by the soldiers of Allah who love war, live by their own [Sharia] law; and threaten anyone who rejects their faith. A reminder of Gen. 12:3a! [1]

Formerly governed by the Ottoman Empire, Palestine—now Israel—has had a generally friendly relationship with Turkey, a NATO country. Following the peace accords after defeating the Egyptian army and air force during the 1967 War, Israel has generally had a friendly relationship with Egypt. But no more.

America is headed for problems as a result of not supporting Israel. Sen. John McCain and others commented:

> . . . That derogatory "hot mic" comments from President Barack Obama and French President Nicolas Sarkozy about Israeli Prime Minister Benjamin Netanyahu [at the G20 conference] are "indicative of the attitude and policies that this administration has had towards Israel." "I happen to be a great admirer of Prime Minister Netanyahu," McCain said on Fox and Friends. "I've known him for years, and Israel is under more pressure and probably in more danger than they've been since the '67 war and that kind of comment is not only not helpful, but indicative of some of the policies towards Israel that this administration has been part of." . . . Republican National Committee Chairman Reince Priebus also weighed in on Tuesday, saying in a statement, "After hearing President Obama's insensitive comments about

> Israeli Prime Minister Netanyahu last week, Americans are wondering: When will Obama start treating Israel like a strategic ally instead of a personal nuisance? . . . It's shocking that the President of the United States would speak of the leader of America's most important Middle Eastern ally in such a reckless way." . . . McCain and Priebus were referring to reports that during the G-20 summit, Obama and Sarkozy could be heard on an open mic[rophone] complaining about Netanyahu, with Sarkozy calling the Israeli leader a "liar and Obama responding, "You're sick of him, but I have to deal with him every day." Reuters reported that Sarkozy also said, "I cannot bear Netanyahu." [2]

The attitude of the current U.S. president has publically been dismissive of Israel and clearly disrespectful of Prime Minister Benjamin Netanyahu. Given the Lord's statement to Abraham in Genesis, America is subject to God's curse as long as we are stepping back from or openly rejecting being Israel's friend (Gen. 12:3).

David Jeremiah sums the situation up well as he writes,

> . . . People who stand in the way of Israel's prosperity—and thus to humanity's blessings—will find themselves standing in the direct path of God's purposes for Israel on earth. And history gives us the tragic story of what happens to anyone, individually or nationally, who puts himself in that unenviable position.
>
> It is no more complicated than that. God created a people for Himself in order to bless the human family. And He will bless those who bless His people—Israel, or the Jews. Those who stand in the way of Israel, not to mention persecute Israel; will find themselves experiencing the judgment of God.[3]

Diplomatic relations damaged

Turkey

As a result of Israel intercepting a so-called humanitarian flotilla which ostensibly was attempting to convey humanitarian supplies to the Palestinians in Gaza, Turkey demanded an apology and, not getting an apology of sufficient veracity, subsequently expelled the Israeli ambassador. The *New York Times* reported in Sept. 2011:

> Turkey said Friday that it was downgrading its diplomatic and military ties with Israel and expelling its ambassador in a display of anger at Israel's refusal to apologize for a deadly commando raid last year on a Turkish ship bound for Gaza . . . Foreign Minister Ahmet Davutoglu said Turkey would reduce its diplomatic representation in Israel to the level of second secretary—one of the lowest diplomatic ranks—and had ordered Israel's ambassador, Gabby Levy, to leave Turkey by Wednesday. The move stopped short of a complete breach in diplomatic relations but nonetheless seemed likely to deepen the already serious alienation between the countries and to further isolate Israel in the region as Arab Spring revolts threaten to undermine other previously stable relationships there. [4]

Egypt

The *New York Times* also reported on the aftermath of the successful Arab Spring protests in Cairo:

> With its Cairo embassy ransacked, its ambassador to Turkey expelled and the Palestinians seeking statehood recognition at the United Nations, Israel found itself on Saturday increasingly isolated and grappling with a radically transformed Middle East where it believes its options are limited and poor. [5]

Palestinians

Since the request for a unilateral declaration of statehood by Hamas and possible ratification by the *United Nations* (UN) of a Palestinian state, peace negotiations have been difficult. The Israelis, under Benjamin Netanyahu, have resisted and outright rejected a return to the pre-1967 boundaries proposed by the Palestinians. Currently, the proposal is on hold in the UN.

In the future

Undoubtedly, nations ignorant of God's protection of Israel will try repeatedly to attack and overcome her. Scripture warns of two such attempts:

The prophet Ezekiel wrote of a group of nations that would attack Israel, "whose people were gathered from many nations to the mountains of Israel," and themselves be overcome by God's "hot anger" (Ezek. 38:8, 18).

John recorded the words of an angel about a great battle in the valley called Har Megiddo (Armageddon) in central Israel in which Jesus (the rider on the White Horse) would win victory over the marauding armies (Rev. 19:19-20).

Iran has threatened for many years to annihilate both the *Great Satan* (United States) and the *Little Satan* (Israel).

Iranian President Mahmoud Ahmadinejad has made and continues to make threats against Israel:

> In a October 26, 2005 address to 4,000 students at a program titled, 'The World Without Zionism', Ahmadinejad said, "Israel must be wiped off the map . . . The establishment of a Zionist regime was a move by the world oppressor against the Islamic world . . . The skirmishes in the occupied land are part of the war of destiny. The outcome of hundreds of years of war will be defined in Palestinian land."

> In a April 14, 2006 speech at the opening of the "Support for the Palestinian Intifada" conference on April 14-16 hosted in Tehran, Ahmadinejad said, "The Zionist regime is an injustice and by its very nature a permanent threat. Whether you like it or not, the Zionist regime is heading toward annihilation. The Zionist regime is a rotten, dried tree that will be eliminated by one storm."
>
> As quoted August 4, 2006 by Malaysian news agency Bernama website, President Ahmadinejad said, "A new Middle East will prevail without the existence of Israel."
>
> In a June 3, 2007 speech, Ahmadinejad was quoted by the Fars News Agency, "With God's help, the countdown button for the destruction of the Zionist regime has been pushed by the hands of the children of Lebanon and Palestine . . . By God's will, we will witness the destruction of this regime in the near future."

Ahmadinejad was quoted by the Fars News Agency on October 10, 2009, "The Zionist regime wants to establish its base upon the ruins of the civilizations of the region. The uniform shout of the Iranian nation is forever 'Death to Israel'."

> In an April 20, 2011 address to a large crowd in the Iranian city of Sanandaj, Ahmadinejad said, "They say they want to create a new and greater Middle East under the U.S. and the Zionist regime's (Israel) dominance. I am telling you that a new and greater Middle East will be established without the existence of the U.S. and the Zionist regime . . . . In recent years, regional nations have realized that the United States and the Zionist regime are their main enemies . . . . Arrogant powers try to deceive nations. They have put the Iranian nation under pressure to oblige it to retreat but the

> resistance of Iranians and their steadfastness has led to their (the West's) defeat." [6]

It seems that, as Iran grows closer to development of nuclear weapons, and despite their constant denial of that goal and assertion that they only want nuclear power for peaceful purposes, Iran's president is consistent in fomenting unrest in the Middle East through his rhetoric. He has arrogated his position to the highest in Iran, yet in reality, while:

> In theory, the president's powers are second only to those of the Supreme Leader, a post occupied by Ayatollah Ali Khamenei since 1989. In practice, his freedom of action is also curtailed by a range of unelected bodies mostly controlled by hard-line [sp] clerics. These bodies, including the Guardian Council, have backed President Mahmoud Ahmadinejad since he was elected in 2005, but thwarted his reformist predecessor Mohammad Khatami. [7]

But God . . . !

CHAPTER 8

Peace in the Middle East

1 A song of ascents. Of David. I rejoiced with
those who said to me, "Let us go to the house
of the LORD." 2 Our feet are standing in your
gates, O Jerusalem. 3 Jerusalem is built like a
city that is closely compacted together. 4 That
is where the tribes go up, the tribes of the
LORD, to praise the name of the LORD
according to the statute given to Israel. 5 There
the thrones for judgment stand, the thrones of
the house of David. 6 Pray for the peace of
Jerusalem: "May those who love you be secure.
7 May there be peace within your walls and
security within your citadels." 8 For the sake of
my brothers and friends, I will say, "Peace be
within you." 9 For the sake of the house of the
LORD our God, I will seek your prosperity.
(Ps. 122 NIV)

People, for a variety of reasons or motivations, want to see peace in the Middle East:

- Some because they want cheap oil again.
- Some because of personal naiveté want to see a lessening of tensions in the region.
- Others for religious reasons desire unity.

As discussed in the previous chapter, throughout her history, Israel has been surrounded with enemies. The entire region has hosted countless battles. Christ's words warning of "wars and rumors of wars" is not a new concept for the Middle East. Jesus said not to worry because these things must happen before the end comes (Matt. 24:6).

Scripture records that there will be an end-times leader who will enter into a seven-year treaty with Israel and usher in the long-sought peace accord, which will however, be revoked midway through the seven years (Dan. 9:27).

The Middle East has long been the venue for conflict. From the ancient civilization of the Sumer, through the Akkadians, Mesopotamians, Chaldeans, Babylonians, Persians, Medes, Greeks and Romans to the time of Christ's birth in Canaan, civilizations in the region have been in conflict.

While there are periods of relative peace, on the whole, peace has been a foreign concept in the region. From a Judeo-Christian standpoint, after God's call to Abram (i.e. later Abraham) to travel from Ur of the Chaldeans to Canaan, Abram and his wife, Sarai (i.e. later Sarah) were found to be unable to have children (Gen. 11:29-12:3) and conflict crept in.

Abram and Sarai took matters in their own hands and used Sarai's servant, Hagar, as a surrogate. The child Ishmael, father of the Arab people, resulted from the union and his descendants have caused Abraham and Sarah's natural child, Isaac, and their descendants—the Jews—much pain to this day. Conflict between Jew and Arab has been the rule rather than the exception. And it's only going to get worse as the final end-times approach.

Ezekiel 38 & 39 forecasts that a leader called Gog, prince of the land of Magog and ruler of Meshech and Tubal, will get an idea, planted by God, to attack the land of Israel as part of a coalition of nations, but that his plans will be thwarted and the members of the coalition destroyed. In Chapter 17, we will discuss the vultures and other birds and animals God will employ to clean up after the carnage of the attacking nations. (Ezek. 38:1-39:16)

In John's Apocalypse, the Lord said regarding a battle in a place called Armageddon that will result in so many dead that, again, God will issue and invitation to the birds of the air to clean up after the conflict. (Rev. 19:17-18)

In the meantime, conflicts continue to plague the region:

- 1948 to this year—Attacks against Israel were discussed in the previous chapter.
- 1990—Saddam Hussein attacked Kuwait to re-annex the country to Iraq.
- 1991—A United Nations (U.N.) coalition led by the United States (U.S.) responded to Hussein's aggression by attacking the Iraqi armies and substantially destroying their effectiveness.
- 2001—al Qaeda terrorists attacked the U.S. in New York, Washington, D.C. and Pennsylvania, resulting in a response of a counterattack in Afghanistan to destroy the al Qaeda terrorist's strongholds there and root out the Talibs and tribal leaders who harbored them.
- 2003—Following reports of weapons of mass destruction (WMD) being prepared by Iraq to use in attacking Israel and the U.S., the U.S. again went back into Iraq to discover and destroy the WMD and liberate Iraq from Hussein's rule.

Joel Rosenberg uses the term *epicenter* for the region surrounding Israel. Just as in an earthquake, an epicenter describes the center or source of activities generating the movement of land or events that ultimately affect the world at large. News media near the turn of the millennium were describing the events taking place in the Middle East as a *political earthquake*, prompting Rosenberg to term the region the *Epicenter.* [1]

Arab Spring

In 2010, the world learned of the flowering of an Arab protest movement called *Arab Spring.* The movement originated in Tunisia in December 2010 and quickly took hold in Egypt, Libya, Syria, Yemen, Bahrain, Saudi Arabia, and Jordan. In the generally autocratic, authoritarian Arab world protest was uncommon. The *Arab Spring* movement emerged from the ethos of the Iraq war as a desire for Western-friendly democracy and was fueled by ubiquitous social media: Facebook, Twitter, and the Internet. Some governments attempted—without substantial success, except in the short-term—to curtail the social media by restricting Internet access within their borders.

Iranian Rhetoric

With the assessment by the *International Atomic Energy Agency* (IAEA) that Iran is definitely developing a nuclear weapons program, in response, Iran has turned up the rhetoric with threats against *North Atlantic Treaty Organization* (NATO) radar installations in Turkey:

> Iran will target NATO's missile defense installations in Turkey if the U.S. or Israel attacks the Islamic Republic, a senior commander of Iran's powerful Revolutionary Guard said Saturday.
>
> Gen. Amir Ali Hajizadeh, the head of the Guards' aerospace division, said the warning is part of a new defense

> strategy to counter what he described as an increase in threats from the U.S. and Israel.
>
> Tensions have been rising between Iran and the West since the release of a report earlier this month by the International Atomic Energy Agency that said for the first time that Tehran was suspected of conducting secret experiments whose sole purpose was the development of nuclear arms. [2]

Israel has been threatening for several years to do a preemptive military strike on Iran's nuclear program and destroy its capability. An August 2010 article in *Haaretz* reported Prime Minister Netanyahu saying:

> "The greatest danger facing Israel and the world is the prospect of a nuclear armed Iran. Iran threatens to annihilate Israel, it denies the Holocaust, it sponsors terror in South America and Afghanistan and Iraq," Netanyahu said Monday. "This is what Iran is doing without nuclear weapons; imagine what it would do with them. Imagine the devastation its terror proxies, Hezbollah and Hamas and others, would wreak under an Iranian nuclear umbrella." [3]

To date (December 2011), Israel has made no overt attacks on Iran, but only God knows what will happen tomorrow; maybe covert efforts to disable the Iranian nuclear or continued urging of world powers to bring pressure on Iran to stop developing a nuclear weapon. The latter is unlikely, given the mindset of the current Iranian leadership.

On December 27, 2011 Iran threatened to close the Straits of Hormuz, shutting off that seaway to oil transport from the Persian Gulf if global sanctions against Iran for nuclear development did not stop. *MoneyNews* reported:

> Iran threatened on Tuesday to stop the flow of oil through the Strait of Hormuz if foreign sanctions were imposed on

> its crude exports over its nuclear ambitions, a move that could trigger military conflict with economies dependent on Gulf oil.
>
> Western tensions with Iran have increased since a November 8 report by the UN nuclear watchdog saying Tehran appears to have worked on designing an atomic bomb and may still be pursuing research to that end. Iran strongly denies this and says it is developing nuclear energy for peaceful purposes.
>
> Iran has defiantly expanded nuclear activity despite four rounds of UN. sanctions meted out since 2006 over its refusal to suspend sensitive uranium enrichment and open up to U.N. nuclear inspectors and investigators.[4]

Regional oil producing nations and analysts seem to think the threat is hollow because it would also negatively affect Iran—in effect, shooting itself in the foot.

Unilateral Declaration of a Palestinian State

Palestinian Authority Prime Minister Salam Fayyad, speaking to *Haaretz*, stated, "Next year, the birth of a Palestinian state will be celebrated, as a day of joy by the entire community of nations.'"[5]

By September 2011, a vote in the UN Security Council was immanent with several members in favor of the application.[6] President Obama waffled on the subject with what many feel was a lame reason. Mr. Obama said,

> The international community should keep pushing Israelis and Palestinians toward talks on the four intractable issues that have vexed peace negotiations since 1979: borders of a Palestinian state, security for Israel, the status of Palestinian refugees and the fate of Jerusalem, which both sides claim for their capital.[7]

By November 2011, the vote was postponed for lack of support by the world community.[8]

The issue of a Palestinian state will not likely disappear anytime soon. At issue are the proposed borders, Israeli security, status of Jerusalem, and the fate of Palestinian refugees in Lebanon, Jordan and Egypt.

Finally

The current threats likely fall under the category of, "You will hear of wars and rumors of wars, but see to it that you are not alarmed. Such things must happen, but the end is still to come" (Matt. 24:6).

But God . . . !

CHAPTER 9

One World Government

> [31] "*His armed forces will rise up to desecrate the temple fortress and will abolish the daily sacrifice. Then they will set up the abomination that causes desolation.* [32] *With flattery he will corrupt those who have violated the covenant, but the people who know their God will firmly resist him.* (Dan. 11:31-32 NIV)

A call for one person or body to govern the world and move to a world money system is growing. Some say we are no longer just nations, but a global society. These are evidencing a shift in thinking from nationalism to globalism. Schools from K through 16 are heavily influencing this shift in thinking. [1]

Even the Vatican is getting their voice heard:

> Blaming the world's economic and financial crisis on an "economic liberalism that spurns rules and controls," the Vatican on Monday (Oct. 24) released an ambitious

> proposal for global regulation of the financial industry and the international money supply . . . The 16-page document from the Pontifical Council for Justice and Peace calls for a "central world bank" to regulate the "flow and system of monetary exchanges similar to the national central banks," such as the U.S. Federal Reserve . . . The proposal also calls for a global tax on financial transactions, whose revenue would go to a fund to help "support the economies of the countries hit by crisis." . . . Ultimately, the plan would help establish a "world political authority" envisioned by Popes John XXIII in 1963 and Benedict XVI in 2009. That body would have international governance on arms control, migration, food security, and environmental protection.[2]

This kind of thinking and wishing for one political body to rule the diverse cultures and countries of the world is the kind of thinking that will usher in the reign of the Antichrist for the final days until God's wrath is complete.

The point is not that one world government is here, but that there is strong international support and initiatives pulling in that direction. The "World Economic and Social Survey" completed in 2010 highlights a number of recommendations.

World Economic and Social Survey (WESS) 2010

The United Nations (UN) WESS 2010 has embodied in it a number of initiatives that will, if fully implemented, move the world closer to a one-world government. The section entitled, "Times are changing," lists four aspects of the world economies and governance occurring today:

- First, there are important ***shifts*** taking place ***in the global economy***.
- Second, ***demographic changes*** in the coming decades will ***strongly influence increasing global interdependence***.

- Third, the ***growing world population*** has been ***supported in part by the degradation of our natural environment***.
- Fourth, ***economic processes*** are ***increasingly interconnected globally***.

> The question is how to reform the institutions responsible for global governance so as to make them better equipped to address these challenges coherently while allowing nations and people to have the space needed to determine their own destinies. [3]

Joshua Goldstein, in *Winning the War on War: The Decline of Armed Conflict Worldwide*, puts forth the proposition that world conflict has declined by virtue of the efforts of the United Nations. His hypothesis is that world governments should submit to the leadership of the UN. Goldstein suggests a new global identity:

> The progress that humanity has made toward ending war has come about not through inevitable, natural, or magical changes, but through the long, hard work of people seeking peace. The job is not finished. However, not only have the number and size of wars decreased in recent years, but our concept of war and military force is changing. The job of soldiers used to be, and still is to some extent, to kill and destroy. Nowadays, however, their job is, as often, to build and protect . . . . The main focus of this book, as of UN peacekeeping itself, is on actions by the international community to end wars and keep them from restarting. [4]

As a staunch advocate for UN global leadership Goldstein states unequivocally those UN methods were not flaws, but rather, features sure to succeed:

> Some observers find the UN too "state-centric" to respond to the challenges of our time. Many critics of the UN point out that it is not democratic. The UN does not consist

> of the people of the world, but of the states of the world, the national governments. Large and small countries get treated equally, and on the other hand permanent Security Council members get preferential status denied to other large, important countries. These criticisms miss the point. These are not flaws in the UN system but innate elements of its design. It would not work without them.[5]

When questions of sovereignty arise, the UN:

> Recognizes each member state's sovereignty on its own territory, over the years a counter concept has developed, that there are limits to sovereignty when governments commit mass atrocities against their own people.[6]

> The UN Charter says, "Nothing contained in the present Charter shall authorize the United Nations to intervene in matters which are essentially within the domestic jurisdiction of any state." However, this principle is trumped by the enforcement measures allowed under Chapter VII when the Security Council acts on a threat to international peace and security. Thus, in practice, the international community can infringe sovereignty by declaring an internal situation—presumably a serious one such as genocide or massive starvation—to constitute a threat to international peace . . . . "Humanitarian intervention" includes robust peace enforcement missions as well as traditional military interventions undertaken for humanitarian reasons, and even, in some definitions, nonmilitary actions such as economic sanctions and criminal prosecutions.[7]

> Norms regarding human rights have evolved in recent decades. Traditionally, notwithstanding Bass's observations about the nineteenth century, human rights have been considered "a profoundly national, not international, issue." During the Cold War, "it was widely accepted . . . that the

> use of force to save victims of gross human rights abuses was a violation of the [UN] Charter." But "a new norm of UN-authorized humanitarian intervention developed in the 1990s." In 1999, Secretary-General Kofi Annan supported the concept of humanitarian intervention if "fairly and consistently applied." He told the General Assembly, "The state is now widely understood to be the servant of its people, and not vice versa." The concept of humanitarian intervention was consistent with the spirit of the UN Charter, he argued.[8]

Goldstein advocates for a one-world government embodied in the UN:

> Today, peacekeeping stands as the most important symbol of the UN, represented in the public imagination by "the symbolic artifacts of peacekeeping—images of blue berets, white vehicles with large black UN letters painted on them, and, of course, the United Nations flag . . . ." However, the view of the UN as a moral force for good has been challenged by a myth of the UN as "an inefficient, ineffective, corrupt, and bureaucratically moribund institution." Bureaucratic and inefficient it may be, but the UN is not only a moral force but our moral force. It belongs to all of us—Americans especially—and we should let nobody steal it from us.
>
> The UN is both an ideal of what the world can be, and a practical tool for bringing us closer to that ideal.[9]

United Nations or another group of nations

In 1970, when the popular book, *The Late Great Planet Earth* by Hal Lindsay came out in bookstores, it was a commonly accepted idea that Lindsay had it right that the emerging European Common Market would be the basis for a reemerging Roman Empire—Daniel's *fourth kingdom* describing the *fourth beast* who will rule over ten heads that are ten kings—representing nations (Dan. 7:23-24a).[10]

At the time, the European Common Market was almost made up of a group of ten European nations. As time has passed, the European Union—formerly the European Common Market—has now grown to twenty-seven nations, with two more waiting in the wings for inclusion, and thus clearly could not be Daniel's *ten heads.*

So who is it? The United Nations is a world body, but has 193 members—far too many to qualify for a ten-nation *fourth kingdom.* This end-times kingdom will logically then, be made up of a group of ten world nations, drawn from nations formerly part of the Roman Empire and in a position to function as Daniel's *ten heads.*

Examining Daniel's prophetic book, Mark Hitchcock draws parallels between Daniel 2 and 7. He finds:[11]

World Empire	**Daniel 1**	**Daniel 7**
Babylon	Head of gold	Lion with the wings of an eagle
Media-Persia	Chest and arms of silver	Lopsided bear with three ribs in its mouth
Greece	Belly and thighs of bronze	Leopard with four wings and four heads
Rome	Iron	Beast with teeth of iron and claws of bronze
Reemerging Roman Empire	Iron & clay	Ten horns and the little horn

It is likely that the ruler which Daniel called the *fourth beast* will be the leader—the *little horn* or Antichrist—who enters in to a seven-year peace treaty with Israel that quiets down the Middle East enough for Israel to build the Third Temple in Jerusalem on the Temple Mount currently housing the Islamic Dome of the Rock and al Aksa Mosque. (See Chapter 18 for more discussion of the Third Temple.)

This group of nations will be powerful enough to overshadow the UN and other world governing bodies, setting the pace for the Tribulation and operating as a one-world government.

Hitchcock says, "This final form of the Roman Empire will evidently begin as some form of democracy and then progress to a dictatorship—just like the Roman Empire began as a republic and eventually became a dictatorship ruled by Caesar."[12]

The truth of this may be found in Rev. Chapters 6, 8, 9, 11 and 16 as we read of the judgments embodied in the seals, trumpets and bowls.

The rider of the white horse is described as holding a bow, but is riding out as a conqueror bent on conquest after receiving a crown symbolic of power. Things get progressively worse with the arrival of the red horse and its rider which have the power to stir up passions in men, who then kill one another. The black horse and its rider bring economic chaos. The pale horse and its rider bring famine and death through plague and animal attacks. It gets worse from that point. The last half of the Tribulation is rightly termed, the Great Tribulation because of its intensity and destruction.

Note that these events start off with firm, but seemingly sloppy leadership and then progresses to autocratic, and finally, despotic control.

By the middle of the Tribulation, the *little horn* (Antichrist) has been killed and resurrected and who then desecrates the Temple. See Chapter 21 for more details.

Information Age

Clearly we are in an age of information. Check out these statistics collected by Steve Wojtowecz, (VP) of Storage Software Development at IBM:

- "The combined amount of tablet and smartphone traffic is predicted to generate 2.7 exabytes of data per month in 2015. That's nearly 3 times all the mobile data generated in the U.S. in 2010.

- More than 75% of the data in the world today was created in the last two years.
- Facebook allows users to share 30 billion pieces of content each month. Twitter's active user base generates 140 million tweets per day. Combined, these sites create 17 terabytes of data every day.
- IDC states nearly 75% of the data that exists today is a copy.
- For those wondering how big a zettabyte is, it is equal to 1 trillion gigabytes or 1,000 exabytes or about 250 billion DVDs."[13]

Eric Savitz of Seagate Technology reported on a *Forbes* article by Steve Wojtowecz:

> Information is power, and having it at your fingertips is a reality in today's smartphone obsessed world.
>
> A recent report by the Pew Internet & American Life Project shows more than 35% of U.S. adults own Smartphones. More compelling is that one out of four smartphone owners do online tasks through their mobile device rather than a computer.[14]

Mark Wojtasiak, Senior Manager, Product Marketing for Seagate Technology noted about the amount of data held by the American government and governments of other nations:

> Governments need to unlock their information vaults, it might just create jobs.
>
> It's true. Why are we collecting the mountains of data in the first place? Today, I would argue that it's a "you never know when you'll need it" mentality. Government regulation requires companies to hang on to data and secure

> it, and governments do the same. Sure there is some analysis done, but think about how much more could be done when the power of the data is fully leveraged by people that know how to mine it. Data has become a natural resource, a new global currency, and by making it available, we may just create a new era . . . scrap the Information Age . . . information is the offspring of Data. What we need is a Data Age, and we need it now.[15]

If one dwells on such things, the idea of governments having so much power can be at least daunting, if not outright terrifying. What could a one-world ruler do with that data?

Antichrist

End-times author Mark Hitchcock sets a standard for consideration of the coming Antichrist that cautions:

> . . . We must be careful not to interpret prophecy in light of current events, but rather, view current events through the lens of Scripture. Looking at biblical prophecy through the headlines is often called "newspaper exegesis" and can lead to unwarranted conclusions and sensationalism.[16]

I am in total agreement with Hitchcock in this caution. However, having said that does not invalidate the exercise of becoming aware of current events and assessing them in light of scripture.

Today, one must keep a Bible alongside one's reading chair to enable putting the puzzle pieces of news and prophecy together, while avoiding the temptation to read more into events than is warranted. Paul the apostle reminded the Ephesians that he had; "not hesitated to proclaim to you the whole will of God" (Acts 20:27 NIV). The Greek word translated "will" is boulen, which means "plan, purpose or motive." [17]

Arrival of the Antichrist

Hitchcock lists five things that are associated with the arrival of the Antichrist:

- **Regathering of Israel**. Israel must exist to enable a treaty to be signed with Israel.[18]
- **Reuniting of the Roman Empire**. Antichrist will arise to rule from a renewed Roman Empire.[19]
- **Globalism**. "The growing consensus among world leaders seems to be that only a consolidation and concentration of power will save the globe from economic disaster and self-destruction."[20]
- **Rebuilt Temple** [in Jerusalem]. Hitchcock says, ". . . that this third Temple has to be built ***before*** Antichrist rises to power because he will make a treaty with the Jewish people that evidently gives them access to the Temple so they can reinstitute and carry out the sacrificial system," citing Daniel 9:27.[21] To some degree, he is right, particularly if his mention of *rises to power* refers to the mid-Tribulation. However, I think it more likely that, ***after*** the Antichrist rises to power sufficient to enter into a treaty with Israel, the way will be open to construction of the third Temple.
- **World outcry for peace**. "The idea of a peace imposed upon Israel by a confederation of Western nations seems like a very probable scenario today."[22]

Livelihood of the Antichrist

The Antichrist will come in like a lamb and will seem to be the realization of many people's hopes and dreams for resolution of the world's political and economic problems. In the end, he will leave like a (conquered) lion. Hitchcock suggests:

> The career of the Antichrist will rise and fall much like a Roman candle lit up on the Fourth of July. He will start out with great fanfare and streak brightly across the skyline of world politics and economics. Then he will explode in a great burst of power and dominion for three-and-a-half years. And at the end, he will fizzle out under the withering judgment of Christ at His second coming. His career, while brief, will be filled with stunning successes and staggering setbacks. The world will have never seen anyone like him.[23]

Likely following the chaos resulting from the *rapture*, the Antichrist will emerge from the rebuilt Roman Empire and seem to be the logical candidate for facilitating the resolution of global problems. He will rise up to shoulder world political power in a time of great crisis. The people of the world will ask, "Where have you been all our lives?"

As he settles in to rule, his true character will emerge and gradually reveal his treachery.

At mid-Tribulation, as the *beast from the sea*, he will die and be resurrected—filled with Satan (Rev. 13:2b-8). People will worship him and Satan. His side-kick, the *beast from the earth*—False Prophet—will demand that all people worship the Antichrist and Satan. The false prophet will also require a mark representing the Antichrist to be placed on people's right hand or forehead so that they may be allowed to buy and sell. Anyone not accepting the mark would be killed (Rev. 13:11-18).

Looking for a Leader

Mark Hitchcock sums up the global leadership crisis well:

> The world today is looking for a leader. With growing dangers and uncertainties everywhere and the global economy spiraling downward, people everywhere are hungry for leadership and direction unlike any other time in human

> history. The world's prospects for the future are gloomy and getting worse. Everyone knows it. And everyone knows that we need someone who can offer hope and chart a clear course for solving the world's mounting crises.[24]

With the right leadership, the world's problems could be solved—or so thinks a large part of the earth's population.

Does America have a Role?

Since its birth in 1776, America has achieved an increasingly important role in world politics. With the passing of the British Empire, the United States of America has risen to a place of world leadership. During the Cold War, most nations considered the United States and the Soviet Union to be the dominant world Superpowers. Following the demise of the Soviet Union, America has become the remaining Superpower in the world, although China is striving to challenge our position.

We played a strong role in the creation of the new Jewish state of Israel in 1948. Pastor and Bible teacher David Jeremiah recounts that,

> America's historic support of Israel is based not so much on efforts by Jewish lobbyists in Washington or the presence of Jewish groups in our society, but on the Judeo-Christian heritage of our nation. President Truman's determination to recognize Israel as a modern state was fueled by his lifelong belief that in the book of Deuteronomy, God had given the land of Israel to the Jewish people for all time.[25]

Prophecy author Thomas Ice is in agreement with Harvard Professor, Barry Fell, Tim LaHaye, Steuart McBirnie, and Mark Hitchcock that, reference to the "merchants of Tarshish and all her villages"—"young lions" in some translations—in Ezekiel 38:13 means that the "villages" cited possibly included the pre-Columbus Americas. Tarshish was home to a world-wide traveling fleet of ocean-going vessels. With so many renowned scholars agreeing, Ice states, "I believe that if America is referenced in Bible prophecy, this passage is the best bet.[26]

Ezekiel 38:13 is written in the context of a coalition of nations which will attack Israel when she is in a time of peace. See Chapter 16 for more discussion of the war of Gog and Magog.

Regarding *Tarshish* and the *villages* or *young lions*, end-times author Mark Hitchcock says:

> Tarshish, on the other hand, is not so simple to identify. At least three locations have been known as "Tarshish" in history. The first was on the east coast of Africa, but the exact location is not known. The second was in England. The third was ancient Tartessus in present-day Spain. The weight of authority seems to favor this third site as the biblical Tarshish—a view supported by both Brown-Driver-Briggs and the Hebrew scholar Gesenius.
>
> Tarshish was a wealthy, flourishing colony of the Phoenicians located in modern Spain that exported silver, iron, tin, and lead (Jeremiah 10:9; Ezekiel 27:12, 25) . . . The NIV cites "her strong lions" as an alternate reading.
>
> The term "young lions" is often used in Scripture to refer to energetic rulers. Therefore, the young lions who act in concert with Tarshish to verbally oppose Gog's invasion could be strong military and political leaders. Another possibility is that "all the young lions" or "all its villages" refers to the nations that have come out of Tarshish.
>
> Where was Tarshish in Ezekiel's day? It was in the farthest west regions of the known world, in Spain. When God commanded Jonah to go preach to Nineveh (about five hundred miles northeast of Israel), Jonah headed to Tarshish or Spain, which was as far in the other direction as he could go (Jonah 1:1-3).

> Tarshish, or modern Spain, could be used by Ezekiel to represent the col-lective nations of Western Europe who will join Saudi Arabia in denouncing Russia's invasion . . . The young lions of Tarshish could be a reference to the colonies that emerged from Europe, including the United States. If this is true, then Ezekiel's young lions of Tarshish describe the last-days United States joining with its European and Saudi–Gulf State allies to lodge a formal protest against the Russian-Islamic aggressors.
>
> If, on the other hand, biblical Tarshish was in England, then the "young lions thereof" could refer to "the United States, Canada, Australia, New Zealand, and other present-day western democracies"—also a clear biblical reference to the role of America in the end times.[27]

America's Christian Heritage

Beginning with our strong Christian heritage growing out of persecution by the established monarchies of Europe, it seemed for a long time, and was commonly accepted by many, to identify the United States as the spiritual replacement for Israel, as described in the Bible. End-times author Terry James when researching for his book, *The American Apocalypse* discovered:

> False teachings about which Jesus and Paul forewarned are at the heart of the delusion that infects Christianity today. The claimed replacement of God's chosen people, the Jews, with Christ's church and with certain nation-states helps make up the matrix of the infection.
>
> Indeed, many have come on the contemporary scene preaching and teaching that today's Israel is not the Israel of God's prophetic Word. These proclaim that the Jews in the world today are not the Jews of God's promises to the patriarchs. The Jews, by race, have, they say, been replaced

> through God's promises to Christians. Christians are the real Jews that are God's chosen people, according to the misguided replacement theologians of these last days.
>
> Some take the matter much further. They declare that the ten tribes of Israel were somehow lost to history but are now found, and the nations of Great Britain and the United States are their homes. These national entities, they say, are now Israel in God's economy of things.
>
> A large majority of the articles and books that popped up when researching for information on the topic of the United States in prophecy were materials distributed by those who claim the Jews of the Old Testament have been replaced by the church, so far as God's prophetic promises are concerned. Also, publishers of the teachings involved in the ten lost tribes being Britain and America turned up in profusion with each search for relevant information.[28]

American theologians seemed to largely agree that it was our destiny to evangelize the world and ring in a new era of global Christianity. For decades, we led the world in missionary activity, eschewing accusations of colonialism from other nations. America was known for its benevolence and Christian-motivated social outreach to lift up less fortunate nations (aka *third world countries*) into a place in the larger community of nations as they forsook paganism and accepted moral Christian values in response to American aid: financial, social, and spiritual.

Theologians began to equate and explain American Christianity as the fulfillment of the Bible prophecies, which speak of Israel's role in the end-times. For example, Christians in America began to look for places they could run and hide during the Tribulation in response to Matthew's, "let those who are in Judea flee to the mountains" (Matt. 24:15-22).

Today, end-times scholars, using a literal interpretation, accept that "Judea" really means Israel and not the United States or other Western nations.

U.S. Constitution

Economist and lawyer Ben Stein, writing in the *American Spectator* in March 2011:

> Maybe I missed something, but wasn't that The Constitution of the United States of America that we just laid to rest this weekend?
>
> It was buried in a private ceremony by Mr. Barack Obama of Chicago, as he silently signed America on to the One World Government some of us have been worried about for decades.
>
> Look at it this way: Where did Mr. Obama get the authority to commit United States forces to war in Libya? There was no declaration of war. There was no authorizing resolution by Congress allowing money to be spent on a war against Col. Gaddafi. As far as I know, there was no meeting of Mr. Obama and top leaders of Congress to discuss the subject in even rough form, let alone detail. There was no lengthy buildup in which the Congress was "allowed" to express the people's opinion on whether we want to be in a third concurrent war.
>
> There was just a vote by the United Nations Security Council, a very far from unanimous vote, and suddenly, the President's Secretary of State, Mrs. Hillary Rodham Clinton, solemnly announced that we were at war.
>
> Meanwhile, again, what . . . happened to the Constitution? Is this Mr. Obama's legacy to our children? The junking of the Constitution in the middle of the night

and the turnover of our sovereignty to the United Nations? (By the way, this is the same UN where Libya until recently sat on the Commission on Human Rights.) Why aren't any questions being asked? Is the Constitution that meaningless to us? Are we that pitiful now? Are we willing to toss overboard the Constitution for the writ of the United Nations? I guess so. Sad days.[29]

One World Government

Google searching for *one world government* brought the following response. In an opinion article posted on the oneworldgovernment.org web site, an anonymous author wrote:

> Let's step outside of religion for a moment and consider matters from the basic secular view of solving the world's major problems. We desperately need, in my opinion, a governing body which is democratic (the United Nations has never been democratic), wholly transparent (think digital fishbowl, in which everybody can see everything), with hundreds of duly-elected (think representative democracy) world parliament members, all elected in free and open elections by their constituents, to legislate on issues beyond the scope of individual nations, without taking any bit of sovereignty away from individual nation states which is justifiably theirs. Basically, take the power to consensually run the world by giving this power to the people of the world. To me it makes perfect sense, and I rather expect that the rest of the world—or most of us, will see things this way once we've considered the matter.[30]

While this opinion was not posted by any recognized authority, it does give one a sense of what some people are thinking today. The oneworldgovernment.org web site says it brings together "informative one world government articles, educational one world government videos, and lively chatter and conversation about one world government in general—both for and against the concept." [31]

On the Internet of course one may read many *facts*; some true, others false; some just fanciful opinion, others founded on solid research. It requires wisdom and discernment to sort out the *facts*. As always, reference to scripture allows one to know which is which.

Antichrist-like Behavior

President Barak Obama has done many things that are of a type that the Antichrist will do when he arrives on the scene. Appointment of *czars* over many aspects of American life thus circumventing the confirmation process normally employed for the purpose. Commentator Mike Bauer reported in *FrontPageMag*:

> Since his election as President, Barack Obama has appointed approximately three-dozen so-called "czars" to manage various governmental responsibilities. These czars have been described as "super aides" who work across agency lines to push the President's agenda. CBS News says they "report directly to Mr. Obama and have the power to shape national policy on their subject area." The lines defining the boundaries of the czars' power are unclear, however, even to many in Congress.
>
> In most cases there are no confirmation hearings to evaluate the qualifications of the appointed czars, thus they are largely insulated from accountability to Congress. [32]

Michael McAuliff reported in a *Huffington Post* blog:

> President Barack Obama had a message for Congress Friday: his so-called "czars" aren't going anywhere.
>
> The budget bill that passed Congress . . . also included a provision to defund a number of White House czars—the high-level presidential appointees whose ranks have

> swelled in recent decades, as a means of skirting Senate confirmation hearings.
>
> There is a long history of complaints about czars by whichever party does not occupy the White House at the time, but the advisers have become a particular target of the right wing during the Obama administration, and the 11th-hour budget deal eliminated his health care, climate, urban affairs and auto-industry czars.
>
> But on Friday night, Obama declared that he intends to ignore that part of the budget legislation, issuing a relatively rare "signing statement" after he inked the budget deal in which he argued that the legislative effort to eliminate those positions was an unconstitutional infringement on the executive branch.
>
> "The President has well-established authority to supervise and oversee the executive branch, and to obtain advice in furtherance of this supervisory authority," Obama wrote in a message to Congress. "The President also has the prerogative to obtain advice that will assist him in carrying out his constitutional responsibilities, and do so not only from executive branch officials and employees outside the White House, but also from advisers within it.
>
> "Legislative efforts that significantly impede the President's ability to exercise his supervisory and coordinating authorities or to obtain the views of the appropriate senior advisers violate the separation of powers," he added. "Therefore, the executive branch will construe [the law as to] not to abrogate these Presidential prerogatives." [33]

These behaviors are just the kind that one can expect from an antichrist in the last days under a one-world government. Barak Obama is not the Antichrist, but is acting as ***an*** antichrist in denying due process and governance to the American people. John instructed believers in 1 John 4:1-6 to:

- Test the spirits.
- The spirits are not from God if they do not acknowledge Jesus came in the flesh.
- Such spirits speak from the world, but not from God.

Obama has waffled both as a candidate and as President about his beliefs. Influences from the likes of Jeremiah Wright, Louis Farrakhan, and the teachings of Muhammad, George Soros, and Bill Ayres formed Obama's pseudo-religious and political views.

A review of the backgrounds of the czars he appointed and still supports reveal a group of:

- communists
- socialists
- homosexuals
- anti-business activists
- anti-gun advocates
- environmental activists [34]

Obama is not alone in his style of antichrist-like leadership. Corruption is rampant in the world: in Europe, Asia, the Far East, and the Middle East. The rebellion of people accompanied by public demonstrations—e.g. *Arab Spring* and *Occupy Wall Street*—clearly shows this. In John 12:18 (NIV), John says, "this is the last hour; and as you have heard that the antichrist is coming, even now many antichrists have come. This is how we know it is the last hour." Some characteristics of an antichrist include:

- An assumption of a mandate to rule.
- Expectations that people will accept his leadership.
- An attitude of "it's my way or the highway."
- Adoption of the Burger King motto, "Have it your way."

- You've got to love me for I am bringing you good.
- Change (to doing it my way) is the best thing that can happen.
- If the laws don't allow me to do things the way I want, we will simply change the laws—or ignore them.

Possible Scenarios

There are a few ways to see the development of a one-world government.

Scenario 1

Iran finally gets the courage to attack the *Great Satan*—United States—and the *Little Satan*—Israel—with nuclear weapons, either as a direct attack using the new long-range missiles they are developing or by supporting terrorist activities (e.g. suitcase nukes, dirty bombs, etc.). In such an event, the United States could be so weakened, militarily and economically, that we are forced to partner with the European Union and support the establishment of a global governing body. It is possible that such an attack on the United States could succeed, given the proclivities of our current national government to emasculate and eviscerate our national intelligence services and military defense. Because of God's warning in Genesis 12:3 of a curse for those who fail to bless Israel, we are vulnerable to such attacks.

Israel, on the other hand, may rely on God's promise to protect them as He has for millennia.

Scenario 2

Politically, the United States may continue to compromise the integrity of its national security and yield to ill-conceived United Nations initiatives such as the UN Convention on the Rights of the Child to allow global legislation to override our sovereignty and mandate the disarming of American citizens, ostensibly with the purpose of protecting children, but in reality with a more central agenda of allowing a central world leader to control the population through threat of military force.

Minority members of the UN have been working feverishly through public information campaigns to convince the majority nations to yield political sovereignty to the UN. Old lessons are often forgotten. Disarming Germany allowed Hitler to manage the population and threaten world nations. Nations which actively disarmed their populations (e.g. Germany, Russia, and Cuba to name a few) acquiesced to being taken over by despots and dictators.

Scenario 3

The great *snatching away—rapture*—occurs and the resultant chaos causes those left to cry out for someone—a global leader—to come and solve the problems remaining after the departure of so many good, ethical, and moral people.

But God . . . !

PART 4

RELIGION

- People, who have previously accepted that personal faith is normal, are now forsaking that belief and are leaving the religious examples of their parents and grandparents.
- Believers in the God of Abraham, Isaac and Jacob are increasingly being persecuted in greater numbers than ever before.
- The seven churches of Asia provide examples of being faithful to Christ as well as unfaithful commitment to God's principles.

CHAPTER 10

Apostasy

> [3] *First of all, you must understand that in the last days scoffers will come, scoffing and following their own evil desires . . . Paul also wrote you with the wisdom that God gave him. . . since you already know this, be on your guard so that you may not be carried away by the error of lawless men and fall from your secure position.*
>
> *(2 Pet. 3:3, 15, 17 NIV)*

Collins *World English Dictionary* defines apostasy as abandonment of one's religious faith.[1]

There will be a great falling away from faith. Through the agency of false prophets; recommending people step back from traditional faith practices (e.g. church attendance, rituals, etc.), and cultural desensitizing, people will be seduced to leave the faith of their fathers and replace God's leadership with other guidance.

Scripture warns that in the last days, men will allow themselves to be carried away by the error of lawless men and so fall away from faith (Matt. 24:10-13). There are signs today that many who previously professed a personal faith in Jesus Christ are actually turning from it.

This phenomenon is particularly pronounced among younger Christians. They may have been influenced by our educational system's liberal leanings toward rejection of religion.

Drew Dyck, in a *Christianity Today* article entitled, *The Leavers*, suggested:

> A Tectonic shift has occurred in the broader culture [in America]. Past generations may have rebelled for a season, but they still inhabited a predominantly Judeo-Christian culture. For those reared in pluralistic, post-Christian America, the cultural gravity that has pulled previous generations back to the faith has weakened or dissipated . . . . A significant part of leaving has to do with the new culture we live in. [2]

A *Pew Forum on Religion and Public Life* poll published in Feb. 2010, reported:

> By some key measures, Americans ages 18 to 29 are considerably less religious than older Americans. Fewer young adults belong to any particular faith than older people do today. They also are less likely to be affiliated than their parents' and grandparents' generations were when they were young. Fully one-in-four members of the millennial generation—so called because they were born after 1980 and began to come of age around the year 2000—are unaffiliated with any particular faith. Indeed, Millennials are significantly more unaffiliated than members of Generation X were at a comparable point in their life cycle (20% in the late 1990s) and twice as unaffiliated as Baby Boomers were

> as young adults (13% in the late 1970s). Young adults also attend religious services less often than older Americans today. And compared with their elders today, fewer young people say that religion is very important in their lives. [3]

The Barna Group's annual study revealed that 31% of those labeling themselves *Christian* are in reality *unchurched*: not attending worship services with any regularity. [4]

From the inception of the United States until the first half of the 20th Century, the predominant religion in America was made up of practicing Protestant or Catholic Christians, except for Jews who mostly practiced their own religion. The United States was a faith-based nation. Even men like Thomas Jefferson, who was himself a deist, respected the righteousness of professing Christians. Missionaries were sent out to the remainder of the world to share the Gospel with those nations and people-groups who had not yet heard.

Beginning in the latter half of the 20th Century, this position of religious strength began to erode. Prayer was taken out of schools; court cases began to arise to remove the legal base of the nation—the Ten Commandments—from public display; homosexuals *came out of the closet*; sexuality and immorality became an increasingly more prominent part of the culture; to name just a few influences moving people to reevaluate their religious values. Church attendance decreased. Yet, apart from some genuine moves of the Holy Spirit, Christians tended to remain aloof from society and culture or gave themselves wholly to it. The Jesus People movement in the 1960s and the advent of seeker-sensitive churches resulted in growth in new ways unknown to mainline Christianity.

It seems God will not long let His people languish. Yet Satan had his victories in seducing some who called themselves Christians to fall into compromise and even outright sin.

People let down their guard against evil and the wiles of the enemy (i.e. Satan) in favor of the false gods of tolerance and political correctness. The words of Solomon, as he pondered his life, moved him to state, ". . . there is nothing new under the sun" (Eccl. 1:9 NIV).

Strangers from Our Midst

Drew Dyck commented in an online article published on *Building Church Leaders:*

> Barna Group estimates that 80 percent of those reared in the church will be "disengaged" by the time they are 29 years old. Unlike older church dropouts, these young "leavers" are unlikely to seek out alternative forms of Christian community, such as home churches and small groups. When they leave church, many leave the faith as well. [5]

Clearly, there remains much work to be done by faithful, committed believers to help their fellow citizens remain faithful to Christ or to just begin and maintain a life of genuine Christian service and ministry.

But God . . . !

CHAPTER 11

Persecution of Believers

> [9] *"Then you will be handed over to be persecuted and put to death, and you will be hated by all nations because of me.* (Matt. 24:9 NIV)

Where formerly tolerance prevailed in many non-Christian parts of the world as a result of recognition of a generally positive value of Christianity, today, native religions opposed to Christian values are increasingly moving their followers to persecute Christians.

Don't think that all persecution takes place solely in foreign lands.

> A local pastor and his wife claim they were interrogated by a . . . county official, who then threatened them with escalating fines, if they continued to hold Bible studies in their home . . . . The county employee notified the couple that the small Bible study, with an average of 15 people attending, was in violation of County regulations, according to their attorney. The attorney reported that, "A few days later the couple received a written warning that listed

> "unlawful use of land" and told them to "Stop religious assembly or apply for a major use permit"—a process that could cost tens of thousands of dollars . . . we believe that the application of the religious assembly principles to this Bible study is certainly misplaced.[1]

This happened in San Diego, California in 2009—Believe it or not! As our nation becomes increasingly secularized, contempt for Christianity will become more widespread. David Jeremiah cited this in *Living with Confidence in a Chaotic World* and warned; ". . . It is indicative of a growing trend in our nation and our world—a trend that requires Christians to be tolerant of everyone and requires no one to be tolerant of Christians."[2]

The 2011 Open Door World Watch List identified a top ten list of countries in which being a Christian is a genuine (and often life-threatening) challenge:

- North Korea
- Iran
- Afghanistan
- Saudi Arabia
- Somalia
- Maldives
- Yemen
- Iraq
- Uzbekistan
- Laos [3]

With the exception of North Korea and Laos which are communist, all of the other eight are Muslim countries. Most of the Islamic countries have Sharia law as their juridical standard and which punish conversion from Islam as a capital crime. The Open Doors International ministry serves persecuted Christians worldwide with Bibles, training and other practical support. Open Doors International yearly produces the World

Watch List, tracking fifty countries that are experiencing significant persecution of Christians.

The persecution has ordinarily taken the form of imprisonment, kidnapping, beatings, general harassment, restriction of liberty, and death.

As the world moves closer to the last days, Christians may expect persecution to be the order of the day and not at all unusual—both in America and world-wide.

A December 2011 article in the *Economist*—based on a study by Pew Research—said:

> Christianity is growing almost as fast as humanity itself, but its 2.2 billion adherents cannot count on safety in numbers. That is partly because the locus of the world's largest religion is shifting to hotter (in several senses) parts of the world. According to a report published by the Pew Forum in December, the Christian share of the population of sub-Saharan Africa has soared over the past century, from 9% to 63%. Meanwhile, the think-tank says, the Christian proportion of Europeans and people in the Americas has dropped, respectively, from 95% to 76% and from 96% to 86%.
>
> But moving from the jaded north to the dynamic south does not portend an easy future. In Nigeria scores of Christians have died in Islamist bomb attacks, targeting Christmas prayers. In Iran and Pakistan Christians are on death row, for "apostasy"—quitting Islam—or blasphemy. Dozens of churches in Indonesia have been attacked or shut. Two-thirds of Iraq's pre-war Christian population has fled. In Egypt and Syria, where secular despots gave Christianity a shield of sorts, political upheaval and Muslim zeal threaten ancient Christian groups. Not all Christianity's woes are due to Muslims. The faith faces

harassment in formally communist China and Vietnam. In India Hindu nationalists want to penalize Christians who make converts. In the Holy Land local churches are caught between Israeli encroachment on their property and Islamist bids to monopolize Palestinian life. Followers of Jesus may yet become a rarity in his homeland.[4]

But God . . . !

CHAPTER 12

Seven Churches Of Asia

> [19] *"Write, therefore, what you have seen, what is now and what will take place later.* [20] *The mystery of the seven stars that you saw in my right hand and of the seven golden lampstands is this: The seven stars are the angels of the seven churches, and the seven lampstands are the seven churches.*
>
> *(Rev. 1:19-20 NIV)*

These churches recorded in John's Apocalypse have been examples of how to and also how not to live as believers.

Prophecy and Bible scholar Chuck Missler suggests, "There were many other churches at that time that would seem to be more historically significant than the seven that Jesus addressed: the churches at Jerusalem, Rome, Galatia, Corinth, Antioch, Colossae, Iconium, Lystra, Derbe, Miletus, to name a few."[1] So why did Jesus choose these seven to address? Was it because they represented the church throughout the ages or did they illustrate specific aspects of a flawed church that He wanted to highlight?

A number of dispensational Bible scholars (e.g. Tim LaHaye, Hal Lindsay, and J. Vernon McGee) suggest a Church Age sequential progression of that age divided into periods characterized by the churches identified in John's vision. Most identify the Church Age as spanning the period from Pentecost to just prior to Daniel's 70th Week—commonly known as the Tribulation Period. [n.b. Most people identifying the Church Age as ending at the *Rapture* hold to a pre-tribulation rapture view.] This may have some historical validity—in that churches through the Church Age exhibit characteristics similar to the seven churches of Asia. However, it is also possible that all of the characteristics of the seven churches exist to some extent in churches today. It may be a breadth issue and not simply a description of the linear-time depth of the Christian church.

Prophecy scholar emeritus John F. Walvoord sums up the common view well:

> Many Bible teachers also believe that the conditions in these seven churches represent the chronological development of church history viewed spiritually. They note that Ephesus seems to be characteristic of the apostolic period in general and that the progression of evil climaxing in Laodicea seems to indicate the final state of apostasy of the church in the last days. There is certainly some merit to this view, although it is a deduction from the text rather than being stated explicitly.[2]

The linear-time view implies that, as each identified stage in time has passed, churches no longer bear those characteristics. For example, the Laodicean Church is marked for its lack of passion for Christ. This is descriptive of many lukewarm or cold churches today.

Various churches in today's world bear the characteristics of one or more of the seven example churches cited by John:

- **Church in Ephesus:** Intolerant of sin and yet, bearing up under persecution (Rev. 2:1-7).
- **Church in Smyrna**: Experiencing afflictions and poverty and about to be severely tested by Satan (Rev. 2:8-11).
- **Church in Pergamum**: Remaining true to Christ's Name, yet being somewhat syncretistic and incorporating pagan beliefs into their worship and practices (Rev. 2:12-17).
- **Church in Thyatira:** Rich in love and faithfulness, yet tolerating Jezebel-like teachings (Rev. 2:18-29).
- **Church in Sardis**: Looking good on the outside, but being dead inside. Asleep at the switch (Rev. 3:1-6).
- **Church in Philadelphia**: Doors open to the gospel and good deeds, yet anemic in their execution (Rev. 3:7-13).
- **Church in Laodicea**: Lost the passion. Could heat up but have chosen not to. Deceived by low standards of living, morality and integrity. Thinking they are well off, but actually not. Have adopted lukewarm, degraded standards of worship and practice (Rev. 3:14-22).

Jesus illustrated aspects of church spiritual life in the citation of these seven churches, commending and warning Christian believers to continue doing the right things and avoid entertaining the wrong things.

A thorough reading of Revelation 2:1-3:22 reveals a message format that is repeated for each of the seven churches. Bible prophecy scholar and academic, Robert L. Thomas identifies the common format of the messages to each of the churches:

1. an *address* opens each letter
2. the citation of *certain attributes of the speaker*
3. an *assertion of complete knowledge* about the people addressed

4. a *description of the state of the church* by way of praise, promise, censure, or warning
5. a promise of *the Lord's coming*
6. a universal *command to hear*
7. a *promise to the overcomer* [3]

The address of each letter is to the *angel of the church.* The word refers to a messenger carrying a communication to the church. The communication is not specifically addressed to the people of the church, except through the messenger.

Jesus differentiates between the angel of the church and the church itself (Rev. 1:12, 16). "The seven stars are the angels of the seven churches, and the seven lampstands are the seven churches" (Rev. 1:20). The word *angel* in Greek refers to an envoy sent to carry a message. It may be a pastor, elder, or even a spirit being. [4]

Contrasting Paul's letter to the Ephesian church and John's Apocalypse, Thomas describes:

> A question [which] has arisen regarding this more "distant" kind of communication. In other words, why did Paul write to the Ephesians (and other cities of Asia, if Ephesians is a circular letter) directly, addressing his words to "the saints" (Eph. 1:1), whereas John wrote his words only to the churches' representatives? Why the difference in intimacy? One explanation is that the more distant style of the Apocalypse is traceable to the low moral state to which the churches of Asia had sunk by the time it was written. Thirty-five years after Paul penned Ephesians, conditions were so deplorable that the Lord could address the churches only through their representatives . . . This explanation reads too much into the method of communication, however. Communication with churches was possible in various ways. There is also the marked difference that Ephesians was written in a complete epistolary form but these seven

> paragraphs are included in one common epistle sent to all seven cities. [5]

These seven churches are but a sample of the possible churches of the region and undoubtedly were chosen for their illustrative value.

Walvoord suggests:

> There has been some debate concerning the theological significance of these seven churches. Clearly, there were many other churches Christ could have selected, including more prominent ones such as Rome, Antioch, Colossae, or even Jerusalem. One reason these seven churches were chosen may have to do with their geographical location in Asia Minor. There is a geographical progression in the order they are presented, beginning at Ephesus, moving north to Smyrna, then farther north to Pergamum, then east to Thyatira, south to Sardis, east to Philadelphia, and southeast to Laodicea. It is also no doubt significant that the number was limited to seven, since this is the number of completeness in Scripture.
>
> It is also obvious that each church the risen Lord addressed needed a particular message to address its particular condition or spiritual need. At the same time, these churches' issues also illustrated conditions that were common in local churches at that time as well as throughout later history. This is why the messages here are applicable to churches in many different settings and historical ages. There are also personal messages of exhortation included, making the messages equally applicable to individual Christians. In fact, each message ends with a personal exhortation beginning with the phrase, "He who has an ear, let him hear." [6]

The bottom line for 21st century Christian churches and congregations is that we must not ignore or pay scarce attention to Christ's warnings, commendations and exhortations to the seven churches. Instead, we must utilize their example to examine our own situation and motivation in the glaring light of Jesus' counsel.

We are seeing many signs of the end times emerge and, as genuine Christians, our personal prerogatives and desires must be obediently subordinated to God's will to be ready for the next great event of time—the *Rapture.* (See Rom. 12:1-3)

But God . . . !

PART 5

SCIENCE & TECHNOLOGY

- Today's environmental concerns as well as misguided, so-called scientific analysis coupled with disasters are causing unfounded fear in the world. God seems to be ramping up changes in the environment beyond those events experienced throughout the ages, as part of the normal environmental cycles.
- Mankind has achieved a pseudo-god-like knowledge through scientific study and research and is now involved in matters which are better left to God.

CHAPTER 13

Environmental Disasters

> [12] *I watched as he opened the sixth seal. There was a great earthquake. The sun turned black like sackcloth made of goat hair, the whole moon turned blood red,* [13] *and the stars in the sky fell to earth, as late figs drop from a fig tree when shaken by a strong wind.* [14] *The sky receded like a scroll, rolling up, and every mountain and island was removed from its place.*
>
> (Rev. 6:12-14 NIV)

Earthquakes in Chili, Japan, Iran caused significant destruction in 2011. The recent tsunami in Japan following the 8.9 magnitude quake displaced over 400,000 people and killed almost 10,000. Damage to nuclear reactors raised fears of a possible nuclear disaster. A sunspot storm on the sun was of a magnitude sufficient to disable electronics worldwide, if it had been aimed directly toward the earth. We ***are*** experiencing warming of the earth, but not caused by humans, as some have mistakenly stated. The warming is historically cyclical in nature, causing the truly uninformed to cry *wolf.*

Black Swan

The *Washington Post* reported on unusual events called *black swans*, "The term *black swan* was coined and popularized by Nassim Nicholas Taleb, a New York University professor of risk engineering and author of 'The Black Swan: The Impact of the Highly Improbable.'" The article goes on to say,

> The disaster bureaucrats talk about black swans: calamities from out of the blue, terrible and strange. The world is now transfixed by the black swan disaster of Japan—an earthquake larger than seismologists thought could happen in that part of the country, leading to a tsunami too big for the sea walls, and now a nuclear crisis that wasn't supposed to be possible.
>
> It may seem as if there are more natural disasters these days, but the real issue is that there are more people and more property vulnerable to the violent forces of Earth. Natural disasters are supplemented by technological disasters—last year's Deepwater Horizon oil spill in the Gulf of Mexico being one example. Disaster planners in the United States have to ask themselves how they would deal not only with the obvious types of calamities—Gulf Coast hurricanes, for example—but also the events that are of low probability but come with high consequences.
>
> "You don't get to pick the next disaster. You don't necessarily know where the threats are," W. Craig Fugate, director of the Federal Emergency Management Agency, said this week as he contemplated Japan's horrific combination of catastrophes. "We plan for the things we know, but we also plan for the things we don't know."[1]

Rare, but not impossible events, might include:

- eruption of a Yellowstone Super volcano

- a megaquake in the Cascadia subduction zone
- a flood of biblical proportions that would turn California's Central Valley into an inland sea
- an electromagnetic pulse (EMP), caused by a solar flare or a terrorist attack, that would knock out the electrical grid for up to 130 million people
- an earthquake could hit an East Coast city not generally considered vulnerable to a major temblor
- earthquakes along the New Madrid seismic zone in the middle United States[2]

World gone wild

The phrase, *world gone wild*, seems to describe well the events of the past two years. A 2010 report about the world gone wild appeared in the December 19 issue of the *Salt Lake Tribune*.[3] The article cited the plethora of environmental events that took place that year, suggesting that the fabled 100-year-[you name it] was exceeded by actual happenings:

- earthquakes
- heat waves
- floods
- volcanoes
- super typhoons
- blizzards
- landslides
- droughts

These environmental events "killed at least a quarter million people in 2010—the deadliest year in more than a generation. More people were killed worldwide by natural disasters this year than have been killed in terrorism attacks in the past 40 years combined."[4]

The article goes on to attribute these incidents to man-caused global warming; a conclusion that is marked by much disagreement within the scientific community.

The *Tribune* article further reported:

> While the Haitian earthquake, Russian heat wave, and Pakistani flooding were the biggest killers, deadly quakes also struck Chile, Turkey, China and Indonesia in one of the most active seismic years in decades. Through mid-December there have been 20 earthquakes of magnitude 7.0 or higher, compared to the normal 16. This year is tied for the most big quakes since 1970, but it is not a record. Nor is it a significantly above average year for the number of strong earthquakes, U.S. earthquake officials say.
>
> Flooding alone this year killed more than 6,300 people in 59 nations through September, according to the *World Health Organization* (WHO). In the United States, 30 people died in the Nashville, Tenn., region in flooding. Inundated countries include China, Italy, India, Colombia and Chad. Super Typhoon Megi with winds of more than 200 mph devastated the Philippines and parts of China.
>
> Through Nov. 30, nearly 260,000 people died in natural disasters in 2010, compared to 15,000 in 2009, according to Swiss Re. The World Health Organization, which hasn't updated its figures past Sept. 30, is just shy of 250,000. By comparison, deaths from terrorism from 1968 to 2009 were less than 115,000, according to reports by the U.S. State Department and the Lawrence Livermore National Laboratory.
>
> The last year in which natural disasters were this deadly was 1983 because of an Ethiopian drought and famine, according to WHO. Swiss Re calls it the deadliest since 1976.
>
> The charity Oxfam says 21,000 of this year's disaster deaths are weather related.

> Super Typhoon Megi not only brought Category 5 winds, but unusually heavily rainfall generated in conjunction with a monsoon system that devastated the northern Philippines and southern Taiwan.[5]

The weird weather and environmental incidents included:

- A volcano [eruption] in Iceland paralyzed air traffic for days in Europe.
- A nearly 2-pound hailstone, 8 inches in diameter, fell in South Dakota in July.
- In a 24-hour period in October, Indonesia got the trifecta of terra terror: a deadly magnitude 7.7 earthquake, a tsunami that killed more than 500 people and a volcano that caused more than 390,000 people to flee.
- After strong early year blizzards—nicknamed Snowmageddon—paralyzed the U.S. mid-Atlantic and record snowfalls hit Russia and China, the temperature turned to broil.

> [The] year started with a good sized El Niño weather oscillation that causes all sorts of extremes worldwide. Then later in the year, the world got the mirror image weather system with a strong La Niña, which causes a different set of extremes. Having a year with both a strong El Niño and La Niña is unusual.[6]

Earthquakes

The synoptic gospels record repeated warnings of earthquakes in the last days (Matt. 24:7; Mark 13:8; Luke 21:11). John the Revelator reports many earthquakes similar to these will take place during the Tribulation Period (Rev. 6:12; 8:5; 11:13, 19; 16:18).

While earthquakes are rather common, especially for those who live in California, they are occurring with greater frequency and magnitude in locations formerly considered relatively earthquake-free.

An article in *Outside* magazine, warns of the likelihood and consequences of a massive mega quake occurring on the Pacific coast of the United States:

> Patrick Corcoran is a professional geographer in Astoria, Oregon, a misty fishing port where the Columbia River meets the Pacific Ocean. By "full-rip nine" Corcoran means a magnitude-9.0 earthquake, the kind of massive offshore temblor that triggered the tsunami that killed 28,050 people in Japan on March 11, 2011. Geologists call them mega quakes. Geologists also call the Northwest coast of North America—from Vancouver Island down to Northern California—one of the likeliest next victims.
>
> Tens of thousands of earthquakes happen around the world every year. Most are too small to be felt. Larger ones—of magnitude 6.0 to 8.0 on the Richter scale—go off nearly every month, but we take notice only when they hit populated targets like cities and schools. The earthquake that leveled Haiti last year was a 7.0. The 2008 quake that collapsed so many school buildings in central China was a 7.9.
>
> Mega quakes, by contrast, are extremely rare. Prior to 2004, scientists hadn't seen one of these 8.5-to-9.5 monsters since the 9.2—magnitude quake that hit Alaska on Good Friday 1964, the second-largest on record. Forty years passed without another one.
>
> Then came Sumatra. Early on the morning of December 26, 2004, a 9.1 earthquake struck off the island's northern coast, creating a tsunami that killed 227,898 people in Southeast Asia. It was the first mega quake in 40 years, but what grabbed the world's attention was the tsunami—in large part because it was the first to occur in the age of digital video.

A second mega quake hit on February 27, 2010, when a 310-mile section of the Pacific plate ruptured off the coast of Chile. The event set off an 8.8 earthquake and generated a tsunami that left 521 dead.

Then, this year, a third mega quake struck off the coast of Japan, which boasts the world's most tsunami-hardened coastline. Cities along the nation's Pacific edge had erected massive protective walls built to withstand tsunamis generated by the largest earthquakes Japan had ever experienced—all in the 8.2-to-8.4 range. The March 11 quake was a 9.0, however, and not even the world's largest seawall, the 1.2-mile, $1.5 billion barrier outside the city of Kamaishi, could hold back the water.

Tom Parsons, a U.S. Geological Survey (USGS) geophysicist at the Pacific Coastal and Marine Sciences Center in Menlo Park, California, say it was chance. "Based on the evidence we've seen," he says, "we don't think that large, global earthquake clusters are anything more than coincidence." Parsons and his colleague, University of Texas at El Paso seismologist Aaron Velasco, studied 30 years of major quakes (7.0 and larger) to see if they triggered subsequent 5.0-plus quakes. They found none.

Parsons's study didn't settle the question. Far from it, in fact. "Make no doubt about it: we're in the middle of a global cluster of mega quakes," says Chris Goldfinger, director of the Active Tectonics and Seafloor Mapping Lab at Oregon State University. "Everybody's noticed it. There are seismologists who say it's not statistically significant. But it's happening. The reason it's downplayed is that nobody's figured out a mechanism—how and why they're happening now."

Goldfinger is no fringe scientist, and what's especially troubling is that this sort of clustering has been seen before.

Six of the world's 16 largest recorded 2 mega quakes happened between 1952 and 1964. More worrying, all six of the '52-'64 cluster mega quakes occurred around the infamous Ring of Fire, the volcano-dotted arc that traces the edge of the Pacific plate. Of the remaining ten largest mega quakes, five have occurred since 2004. All five were along the Ring of Fire.

"Places that were previously considered safe, well, they're now being reconsidered," Goldfinger says.[7]

In late 2010 and 2011, earthquakes hit:

- Oklahoma—[Nov. 5, 2011] . . . the area experienced the strongest earthquake ever recorded in the state [magnitude 5.6] . . . . Geological activity in the region has increased in recent years, and earthquakes have occurred with greater frequency and intensity . . . . Unlike earthquake-prone California and Japan, Oklahoma does not rest atop the fractious areas where two tectonic plates rub against each other. But the state's geophysical activity has only been surveyed in earnest for about 50 years . . . making it difficult to draw conclusions or put the recent activity into context.[8]
- Turkey—7.2-magnitude earthquake struck eastern Turkey.[9]
- Iran—A magnitude 6.5 earthquake struck southeastern Iran late Monday, killing at least six people and injuring 21 others.[10]
- Vancouver, Canada—A 6.4 magnitude earthquake off the west coast of Vancouver Island shook Metro Vancouver and other parts of the province.[11]
- Five significant earthquakes occurred in the Pacific in March 2011:

- near The East Coast of Honshu, Japan—March 9, 2011—magnitude 7.2
- near The East Coast of Honshu, Japan—March 11, 2011—magnitude 9.0
- Vanuatu—March 17, 2011—magnitude 6.3
- near The East Coast of Honshu, Japan—March 22, 2011—magnitude 6.6
- Myanmar—March 24, 2011—magnitude 6.3 [12]

Solar Activity

In October 2011, *ABC News* carried the story of "Red and pink streaks filled the sky across parts of the country after Earth's magnetic field was hit by a coronal mass ejection, enabling the Northern Lights to be seen across the southeastern part of the United States."[13]

There are growing concerns about sun spots—*coronal mass ejections* (CME). Electromagnetic pulses resulting from CME activity could potentially damage large portions of the electronic and electrical circuitry on earth by virtue of the fact that electronic and electric circuits are influenced by magnetic fields.

Society is largely controlled by electronic circuitry today. If circuits (e.g. computers, relays, cell phones, etc.) were burned out by large magnetic pulses, the earth could be thrown back into the dark ages. Our homes, transportation, and communication are all controlled by electronic chips. In February 2011, there was a near miss of such a pulse originating from the confluence of five sun spots that sent a wave of magnetism toward the earth. Because the earth was aligned slightly away from the center of the wave, there was little notice of it. Scientists reported, "With five sunspots rotating at the same time, enough energy has been injected into the [earth's] atmospheric magnetic field to produce the largest solar flare seen for almost five years."[14]

Scientists at NASA have a new tool, the Solar Dynamics Observatory satellite, to predict disruptive solar storms. This satellite allowed NASA scientists to view sunspot activity this year (2011).

> In March, a solar storm created the fastest-traveling CME seen in six years. A wave of particles racing at 5 million mph (8 million kph) shot into space away from Earth. Similarly, around Labor Day in September, the sun erupted with several CMEs and solar flares, including an X-class outburst Sept. 6.[15]

An X-class solar flare is the most powerful type of solar storm. "Scientists classify strong solar flares in three categories: C, M and X, with the X-class being the most powerful. So far in 2011, eight X-class flares have been observed."[16]

Researchers at Reading University in Great Britain say "Within decades, solar storms are likely to become more disruptive to planes and spacecraft. The work, published in Geophysical Research Letters, predicts that once the Sun shifts towards an era of lower solar activity, more hazardous radiation will reach Earth."[17]

Electromagnetic pulses (EMP) can be generated by nuclear explosions as well. Nations are developing EMP weapons to target electronic circuitry in the event of war. While God is responsible for what happens on the sun, man is working to get into the act and disrupt society for his own, not-always-constructive purposes.

Storms

The U.S. Geological Survey organization has made some estimates of what they feel is the likely next great challenge to the West coast of the United States and plans to test disaster preparedness. The current project for 2011 involves, "a winter storm scenario called ARkStorm (for Atmospheric River 1,000)." It is described as:

> . . . [A] large, scientifically realistic meteorological event followed by an examination of the secondary hazards (for example, landslides and flooding), physical damages to the built environment, and social and economic consequences. The hypothetical storm depicted here would strike the U.S. West Coast and be similar to the intense California winter storms of 1861 and 1862 that left the central valley of California impassible. The storm is estimated to produce precipitation that in many places exceeds levels only experienced on average once every 500 to 1,000 years.[18]

In April 2011, dozens of tornados hit six southern states, killing 209 people. An Associated Press article quoted by *Yahoo! News* reported,

> Dozens of tornadoes spawned by a powerful storm system wiped out neighborhoods across a wide swath of the South, killing at least 209 people in the deadliest outbreak in nearly 40 years, and officials said Thursday they expected the death toll to rise.
>
> Alabama's state emergency management agency said it had confirmed 131 deaths, while there were 32 in Mississippi, 24 in Tennessee, 13 in Georgia, eight in Virginia and one in Kentucky.
>
> The National Weather Service's Storm Prediction Center in Norman, Okla., said it received 137 tornado reports around the region . . .
>
> . . . A meteorologist with the prediction center, said the deaths were the most in a tornado outbreak since 1974, when 315 people died.[19]

Disease

Through the ages, mankind has been plagued with a number of virulent diseases, the most common being tuberculosis, malaria, and AIDS.

The following is a list of the 22 most common infectious diseases throughout the world today:

- ***African Trypanosomiasis*** ("sleeping sickness")—spread by the tsetse fly.
- ***Cholera***—spreads mostly through contaminated drinking water and unsanitary conditions.
- ***Cryptosporidiosis***—spreads when a water source is contaminated, usually with the feces of infected animals or humans.
- ***Dengue***—commonly called dengue fever . . . spreads through the bite of the *Aedes aegypti* mosquito.
- ***Hepatitis A***—causes a highly contagious liver disease. Spreads primarily by the fecal-oral route or by ingestion of contaminated water or food.
- ***Hepatitis B***—the most common and most serious infectious disease in the world today. Over 350 million of those infected never rid themselves of the infection. An inflammation of the liver causes symptoms such as jaundice, extreme fatigue, nausea, vomiting, and stomach pain; Chronic infections can cause cirrhosis of the liver or liver cancer in later years.
- ***Hepatitis C***—a less common, and less severe, form of hepatitis. An estimated 180 million people worldwide are infected with hepatitis C virus (HCV); 3-4 million more are infected every year. The majority of HCV cases are asymptomatic, even in people who develop chronic infection.

- ***HIV/AIDS****—Acquired Immune Deficiency Syndrome* (AIDS), was first reported in mid-1981 in the United States; it is believed to have originated in sub-Saharan Africa. The *Human Immunodeficiency Virus* (HIV) that causes AIDS was identified in 1983, and by 1985 tests to detect the virus were available.
- ***Influenza***—Influenza virus attacks the human respiratory tract, causing symptoms such as fever, headaches, fatigue, coughing, sore throat, nasal congestion, and body aches.
- ***Japanese Encephalitis***—is a mosquito-borne disease endemic in Asia. Around 50,000 cases occur each year; 25% to 30% of all cases are fatal.
- ***Leishmaniasis***—a disease spread by the bite of the sandfly. Coalition military personnel serving in Iraq experienced it in Operation Desert Storm and Operation Iraqi Freedom.
- ***Malaria***—a mosquito-borne disease that affects more than 500 million people annually, causing between 1 and 3 million deaths . . . most common in tropical and subtropical climates . . . Most victims are children. Infected people also often suffer from anemia, weakness, and a swelling of the spleen. Malaria was almost eradicated 30 years ago; now it is on the rise again.
- ***Measles***—a disease that has seen a drastic reduction in countries where a vaccine is readily available. Symptoms include high fever, coughing, and a rash; common complications include diarrhea, pneumonia, and ear infections.
- ***Onchocerciasis*** ("river blindness")—caused by the larvae of *Onchocerca volvulus*, a parasitic worm that lives in the human body for years. Symptoms include visual impairment, rashes, lesions, intense itching, skin depigmentation, and lymphadenitis.

- ***Pneumonia***—usually an infection of the streptococcus or mycoplasma bacteria.
- ***Rotavirus***—Rotavirus is the most common cause of viral gastroenteritis worldwide. Symptoms include vomiting, watery diarrhea, fever, and abdominal pain.
- ***Schistosomiasis***—a parasitic disease that is endemic in many developing countries. Symptoms include rash and itchiness soon after becoming infected, followed by fever, chills, coughing, and muscle aches.
- ***Shigellosis***—most common in developing countries with poor sanitation. Symptoms include diarrhea with bloody stool, vomiting, and abdominal cramps.
- ***Strep Throat***—caused by the *streptococcus* bacteria. Symptoms include a sore throat, fever, headache, fatigue, and nausea.
- ***Tuberculosis***—*tuberculosis* (TB) bacteria are most often found in the lungs, where they can cause chest pain and a bad cough that brings up bloody phlegm. Other symptoms include fatigue, weight loss, appetite loss, chills, fever, and night sweats.
- ***Typhoid***—usually spread through infected food or water. Symptoms include a sudden and sustained fever, severe headache, nausea, severe appetite loss, constipation, and sometimes diarrhea.
- ***Yellow Fever*****—**has two phases: "acute phase," symptoms include fever, muscle pain, headache, shivers, appetite loss, nausea, and vomiting . . . most patients recover. 15% will enter the "toxic phase," in which fever reappears, along with other symptoms, including jaundice; abdominal pain; vomiting; bleeding from the mouth, nose, eyes, and stomach; and deterioration of kidney function (sometimes complete kidney failure). Half of all patients in the toxic phase die within two weeks; the other half recover.[20]

The reader will note the absence of *smallpox* in this list, an infectious disease which has decimated mankind for millennia. The *World Health Organization* (WHO) published the following information about smallpox:

> Smallpox is an acute contagious disease caused by *variola* virus, a member of the *orthopoxvirus* family.
>
> Smallpox, which is believed to have originated over 3,000 years ago in India or Egypt, is one of the most devastating diseases known to humanity. For centuries, repeated epidemics swept across continents, decimating populations and changing the course of history.
>
> In some ancient cultures, smallpox was such a major killer of infants that custom forbade the naming of a newborn until the infant had caught the disease and proved it would survive.
>
> In the early 1950s—150 years after the introduction of vaccination—an estimated 50 million cases of smallpox occurred in the world each year, a figure which fell to around 10-15 million by 1967 because of vaccination.
>
> In 1967, when WHO (World Health Organization) launched an intensified plan to eradicate smallpox, the "ancient scourge" threatened 60% of the world's population, killed every fourth victim, scarred or blinded most survivors, and eluded any form of treatment.
>
> Through the success of the global eradication campaign, smallpox was finally pushed back to the horn of Africa and then to a single last natural case, which occurred in Somalia in 1977. A fatal laboratory-acquired case occurred in the United Kingdom in 1978. The global eradication of smallpox was certified, based on intense verification activities in countries, by a commission of eminent scientists

> in December 1979 and subsequently endorsed by the World Health Assembly in 1980.[21]

One would think that there are enough diseases to plague mankind.

On the contrary, enough new diseases keep popping up to let man know that God is still in charge and still hates sin. As previously noted, in the 1980s HIV and AIDS appeared and began its devastation in Africa, then spread to the rest of the world. In recent years, various drug-resistant diseases have developed to complicate medical care.

Methicillin-resistant Staphylococcus aureus (MRSA), termed a *Superbug*, is commonly found in hospitals and healthcare facilities. According to the *Centers for Disease Control* (CDC):

> Antimicrobial—antibiotic—resistance is one of the world's most pressing public health threats.
>
> Antimicrobials include antibiotics, antivirals, antifungals, and other medications used to treat life-threatening diseases. Antimicrobial resistance occurs when germs change in a way that reduces or eliminates the effectiveness of drugs to treat them. Widespread overuse and inappropriate use of antimicrobials is fueling an increase in antimicrobial-resistant organisms (germs). Increased resistance is compromising the effectiveness of these important treatments. As resistance increases, the patient's risk for complications or death from infection also increases.[22]

In 2008, scientists began to warn of further mutation of the Superbugs. MRSA now has two strains: one that lives in hospitals and medical facilities and another that lives in community settings such as sports arenas. A British article published in *The Lancet*, the world's leading general medical journal and specialty journals in Oncology, Neurology and Infectious Diseases, warned of new drug-resistant bacteria in hospitals.[23]

Diseases throughout the ages have killed millions of people. Remember hearing of the Bubonic and Pneumonic Plagues of the middle ages? The Influenza Epidemic of the early 20th Century took more lives than World War I.

John's Apocalypse warns of plague pandemics that will occur during the Tribulation Period. The rider on the pale horse was given power over ¼ of the earth to kill with famine and plague (Rev. 6:8). God allows such things to punish mankind for the sins they have committed. Jewish believers and gentile Tribulation Saints will be protected. Men and women who turn to the Lord in that time will be protected. Those who don't will suffer.

God can choose any form of disease to bring judgment on the world's sinners, but He could also use any of the common infectious diseases that exist today. He is the one who has the detailed plan.

Plagues

Biblical plagues are not limited to disease, but rather include all of the kinds discussed in this chapter. Revelation warns of earthly, cosmic, ***and*** disease plagues taking place during the Tribulation Period.

But God . . . !

CHAPTER 14

Science & Technology

> [4] *But you, Daniel, close up and seal the words of the scroll until the time of the end. Many will go here and there to increase knowledge.*
>
> (Dan. 12:4 NIV)

The prophet Daniel spoke of the increase of knowledge in the last days.

In 2011, people are more informed and scientifically sophisticated than in the days when Jesus walked the earth. For whatever reason, God has allowed man to discover and use technology which would have seemed magic a century ago. Yet the technology is not accompanied by the wisdom to know how to best use it.

Some current projects

Instead, man has developed a sense of arrogance and pride that go counter to God's plan. Studying the stars, scientists think they can control the universe. The Lord has inspired individuals to understand, invent, and develop objects and processes that benefit mankind. On the other hand, man has also developed objects and processes that are used to destroy other men and the environment.

When man goes beyond God's plan (cf. Prov. 16:18) to displace Him, man often errs. Playing God comes with a price! The *Law of Unintended Consequences* rears its ugly head. Just look at the side effects of new drugs that are only later discovered to result in harm to humans and be pulled from the pharmacy shelves.

The U.S. *Defense Advanced Research Projects Agency* (DARPA) BioDesign Project has:

> A goal of eliminating "the randomness of natural evolutionary advancement." The plan would assemble the latest bio-tech knowledge to come up with living, breathing creatures that are genetically engineered to "produce the intended biological effect."
>
> DARPA wants the organisms to be fortified with molecules that bolster cell resistance to death, so that the lab-monsters can "ultimately be programmed to live indefinitely."
>
> Of course, DARPA's got to prevent the super-species from being swayed to do enemy work—so they'll encode loyalty right into DNA, by developing genetically programmed locks to create *tamper proof* cells. Plus, the synthetic organism will be traceable, using some kind of DNA manipulation, "similar to a serial number on a handgun." And if that doesn't work, don't worry. In case Darpa's plan somehow goes horribly awry, they're also tossing in a last-resort, genetically-coded kill switch: *Develop strategies to create a synthetic organism "self-destruct" option to be implemented upon nefarious removal of organism.*
>
> Of course, Darpa's up against some vexing, fundamental laws of nature—not to mention bioethics—as they embark

on the lab beast program. First, they might want to rethink the idea of evolution as a random series of events, says NYU biology professor David Fitch.[1]

Katie Drummond, writing in *Wired* magazine, said:

> The concern that humans might be overreaching when we create organisms that never before existed can be a safety concern, but it also returns us to disagreements about what is our proper role in the natural world (a debate largely about non-physical harms or harms to well-being).[2]

British researchers are calling for stricter rules on experiments involving animal-human tissue:

> Scientific experiments that insert human genes or cells into animals need new rules to ensure they are ethically acceptable and do not lead to the creation of "monsters," a group of leading British researchers said.
>
> Chinese scientists have already introduced human stem cells into goat fetuses and U.S. researchers have studied the idea of creating a mouse with human brain cells—though they have not actually done so.
>
> Using animals with limited humanized traits is not new. Genetically engineered mice containing human DNA are already a mainstay of research into new drugs for diseases like cancer.
>
> But Martin Bobrow, a professor of medical genetics at the University of Cambridge, who led the Academy's working group, said there were three areas of particular concern.
>
> "Where people begin to worry is when you get to the brain, to the germ (reproductive) cells, and to the sort of central features that help us recognize what is a person, like skin texture, facial shape and speech," he told reporters.

> His report recommends that government should put in place a national expert body, working within the existing system for regulating animal research, to oversee such sensitive areas.[3]

The decline in ethics in the global arena could result in some scary results. Imagine some *mad scientist* working to create the kinds of creatures described in Revelation: locusts with animal, human and insect features (Rev. 9:7-10); fire-breathing horses with lion heads and tails like snakes (Rev. 9:17-19).

3-D Printing

Researchers are already working on 3-D printing of human body parts:

> The machine looks like the offspring of an Erector Set and an inkjet printer.
>
> The *ink* feels like applesauce and looks like icing. As nozzles expel the pearly material, layer by layer, you imagine the elaborate designs this device could make on gingerbread cookies.
>
> But the goo is made of living cells, and the machine is *printing* a new body part.
>
> These machines—they're called three-dimensional printers—work very much like ordinary desktop printers. But instead of just putting down ink on paper, they stack up layers of living material to make 3-D shapes. The technology has been around for almost two decades, providing a shortcut for dentists, jewelers, machinists and even chocolatiers, who want to make custom pieces without having to create molds.
>
> In laboratories all over the world, experts in chemistry, biology, medicine and engineering are working on many

paths toward an audacious goal: to print a functioning human liver, kidney or heart using a patient's own cells.

That's right—new organs, to go. If they succeed, donor waiting lists could become a thing of the past.

"The possibilities for this kind of technology are limitless," said Lawrence Bonassar, whose lab at Cornell University has printed vertebral tissue that tested well in mice.

Scientists say the biggest technical challenge is not making the organ itself, but replicating its intricate internal network of blood vessels, which nourishes it and provides it with oxygen.

Many tissue engineers believe the best bet for now may be printing only an organ's largest connector vessels and giving those vessels' cells time, space and the ideal environment in which to build the rest themselves; after that, the organ could be implanted.

The cells, after all, have been functioning within the body already in some capacity, either as part of the tissue that is being replaced or as stem cells in fat or bone marrow. (Donor stem cells could be used, but ideally cells would come directly from the patient.)

"If the federal government created a 'human organ project' and wanted to make the kidney, I literally think it could happen in 10 years," said chemical engineer Keith Murphy, co-founder of Organovo, a firm that makes and works with high-end bioprinters. But that would require a massive commitment of people, resources and billions of dollars, he said.

Once scientists get over the financial and technical hurdles of bioprinting, they will have to square the process

> with the Food and Drug Administration, which will have to decide how to regulate something that is not simply a device, a biological product or a drug, but potentially all three.[4]

Of course, intentions are good in many cases. For example:

> Washington State University researchers have used a 3D printer to create a bone-like material and structure that can be used in orthopedic procedures, dental work and to deliver medicine for treating osteoporosis.
>
> It looks like bone. It feels like bone. For the most part, it acts like bone . . . . The . . . report on successful in vitro tests in the journal Dental Materials and say they're already seeing promising results with in vivo tests on rats and rabbits. It's possible that doctors will be able to custom order replacement bone tissue in a few years, said Susmita Bose, co-author and professor in WSU's School of Mechanical and Materials Engineering.
>
> "If a doctor has a CT scan of a defect, we can convert it to a CAD [*Computer-Aided Drafting*] file and make the scaffold according to the defect," Bose said.[5]

The Mark

The achievements of scientific research are voluminous. One is particularly remarkable because it relates to a long-time concern for Christians—the Mark of the Beast. The book of Revelation reveals that the Antichrist—the Beast from the Sea—and his cohort—the Beast from the Earth (i.e. the False Prophet)—will require all people, who desire to buy or sell anything, to take a mark on their right hand or forehead (Rev. 13:16-17).

There has been much speculation on the form of the mark: tattoo, RFID chip, or . . .

Scripture is not specific as to the actual method and just mentions the location of application. Having said that, in the 1970s, Christians were expecting to receive a tattoo as the mark. From the late 1990s on, the expectation was that the mark would be by *Radio Frequency Identification* (RFID) chips such as are used with pets to track them when lost.

PositiveID, formerly VeriChip Corporation, markets RFID Chips for a number of purposes. The VeriChip system, "uses the first human-implantable passive RFID microchip, cleared for medical use in October 2004 by the United States Food and Drug Administration."[6]

In 2009, VeriChip Corporation and Steel Vault Corporation, merged to become PositiveID. PositiveID provides unique health and security identification tools to protect consumers and businesses.[7]

As far back as 2004, an article in *USA Today*, reported on VeriChip's marketing:

> . . . There's the important and deeply scientific experiment being conducted among the barely clothed patrons of Baja Beach Club in Barcelona. They're getting electronic credit cards implanted under their skin.
>
> Beautiful club-goers have a problem: If you're going to wear a halter top and micro-skirt, there's not much of anywhere to put a wallet. And who wants to carry a purse when you're there to dance? Luckily, a company called VeriChip this year unveiled a solution based on radio-frequency identification (RFID) technology.
>
> It's a slender glass capsule about as long as a dime is wide. Inside sits a computer chip, which stores a unique code that can identify an individual—sort of an electronic Social Security number. The capsule also holds a tiny antenna, which can radio that code to a receiver many feet away.

At the Baja Beach Club, Tuesdays are VeriChip implantation days. Stop in and a *nurse*—the club's word—uses a syringe to inject a VeriChip capsule under your skin. There don't seem to be any rules about where on the body it has to be placed. If you think this sounds like something you'd never do, then you're not the kind of person who goes to clubs wearing your *bestest* nose ring.

Once implanted, you become your own credit card. Need to pay for a drink? Wave your implant near a reader, and you're done. VeriChip has dreams of going global with its "human implantable ID technology"—once implanted, you could wave a body part to pay for a burger at Wendy's, a beer at a baseball game, or whatever.

There are a few kinks to be worked out, like the fact that you can't turn the chip off. Privacy groups are going to dog-pile on that one.[8]

Today, the University of Illinois at Urbana-Champaign reports:

Engineers have developed a device platform that combines electronic components for sensing, medical diagnostics, communications and human-machine interfaces, all on an ultrathin skin-like patch that mounts directly onto the skin with the ease, flexibility and comfort of a temporary tattoo.

The patches are initially mounted on a thin sheet of water-soluble plastic, [and] then laminated to the skin with water—just like applying a temporary tattoo. Alternately, the electronic components can be applied directly to a temporary tattoo itself, providing concealment for the electronics.

Rogers collaborated with Northwestern University engineering professor Yonggang Huang and his group to

> tackle the difficult mechanics and materials questions. The team developed a device geometry they call *filamentary serpentine*, in which the circuits for the various devices are fabricated as tiny, squiggled wires. When mounted on thin, soft rubber sheets, the wavy, snakelike shape allows them to bend, twist, scrunch and stretch while maintaining functionality.
>
> "The blurring of electronics and biology is really the key point here," Huang said. "All established forms of electronics are hard, rigid. Biology is soft, elastic. Its two different worlds. This is a way to truly integrate them."
>
> Next, the researchers are working to integrate the various devices mounted on the platform so that they work together as a system, rather than individually functioning devices, and to add Wi-Fi [*wireless fidelity*] capability.[9]

One commentary, mentioning the Antichrist, by Jim Edwards, reporting for *CBS News*, said:

> The news that Novartis wants a deal with Proteus Biomedical to produce a microchip called "Raisin" that will text your mobile phone when it's time to take another pill, and VeriChip's efforts to link microchip implants to online health records, has caused two separate controversies that seem bound to collide: some Christians believe the devices are eerily similar to the "mark of the beast" as described in the book of Revelation; while "singularity" buffs—those who look forward to the merger of humans and intelligent technology—regard it as a bold step forward in improving health.
>
> The Christians make the obvious argument. On the subject of "the beast," [see] Revelation 13:16-18.[10]

Edwards makes a cogent observation with a parenthetic poor attempt at humor; "The suggestion is that if the government starts requiring chip implants, then this will be a sign that the antichrist is in charge and we're at the end of days. (Of course, the beast in question will have 'two horns like a lamb, and he spake as a dragon,' which should be easy to spot in a presidential candidate.)"[11]

The technology is now in place to allow fulfillment of Rev. 13:16-17 when God decides the time is right.

New technologies are being developed every year. One of the latest has relevance to the mark of the beast—*Near Field Communication* (NFC). This technology is being tested in many countries across the globe. According to Rohde & Schwarz, an NFC enterprise:

> *Near Field Communication* (NFC) is a new short-range, standards-based wireless connectivity technology, which uses magnetic field induction to enable communication between electronic devices in close proximity. Based on RFID technology, NFC provides a medium for the identification protocols that validate secure data transfer. NFC enables users to perform intuitive, safe, contactless transactions, access digital content and connect electronic devices simply by touching or bringing devices into close proximity.[12]

The short range of NFC—~10 centimeters—makes it a relatively secure means of conducting business with minimal fear of information theft. Devices employing this technology include smart phones. Apple Computer is exploring the use of the iPhone as a source of data transfer for banking and other commerce.

An advertisement in *Forbes Magazine* revealed,

> The hottest consumer application for NFC right now is mobile payments. In this scenario, a user's credit card information is stored securely in an NFC-equipped smartphone. To make

> a purchase, the user simply touches the phone to a retail point-of-sale terminal, the two devices share information wirelessly and the transaction takes place.[13]

Further research produced the article cited in reference 12 above. NFC-enabled devices can accomplish eCommerce, building entrance authorization, file-sharing, personal information access, ticketing, boarding passes, keycard for house, car, and office, and instant WiFi configuration. This technology is ripe for someone like the prophesied Antichrist to employ.

So, *tattoo, RFID*, or *NFC device*? Science is now able to provide the means to authorize buying and selling as ordered by the Antichrist.

But God . . . !

PART 6

LAST DAYS

- No study of Bible prophecy and comparison to evolving world events would be complete without reference to the prophesied events of the Last Days.
- Christians are eagerly looking forward with expectation to the *rapture*—whenever it takes place—and there are several opinions about when that will be.
- Timing of the War of Gog and Magog is still being debated by theologians and prophecy scholars.
- One day (twice actually) carrion birds will be invited by God to a feast.
- Jesus Christ will return and split the Mount of Olives.
- For the Antichrist to desecrate it, the Temple must exist.
- Many false messiahs will appear and perform signs and wonders to deceive the world and even believers.
- Daniel prophesied about a seventieth week and John the apostle provides the details of events scheduled for the Tribulation.
- A final battle in which the enemies of God will be ultimately vanquished is scheduled to take place.
- Following the battle and some cleaning up, the world will enter a period of 1000 years of peace and safety.

CHAPTER 15

The Great "Snatching Away"

> [16] *For the Lord himself will come down from heaven, with a loud command, with the voice of the archangel and with the trumpet call of God, and the dead in Christ will rise first.* [17] *After that, we who are still alive and are left will be caught up together with them in the clouds to meet the Lord in the air. And so we will be with the Lord forever.* [18] *Therefore encourage each other with these words.*
>
> *(1 Thess. 4:16-18 NIV)*

There is a growing interest and expectation among Biblically literate Christians in the event commonly referred to as *The Rapture*. There are a number of theories about the timing of this event, but many Christians have a sense that it is on the horizon.

A study, published in June 2011, by the Pew Research Center's *Forum on Religion & Public Life* surveyed over 4000 global evangelical Protestant leaders participating in the Third Lausanne Congress of World Evangelization.[1] The survey found that "about six-in-ten Lausanne Congress participants (61%) believe in the Rapture of the church—the prophecy that as the end of the world draws near, Christians will be instantly taken up to heaven, leaving non-believers behind."[2]

The survey cautions that, ". . . Participants surveyed by the Pew Forum differ in important ways from rank-and-file evangelicals in their home countries. They are predominantly male, middle-aged and college-educated, and nearly three-quarters (74%) are employed by churches or religious organizations. Fully half (51%) are ordained ministers. Hence, the survey results do not necessarily reflect the views of evangelicals as a whole." It should be noted that a significant number of Christians today ***are*** looking forward expectantly to the event known as *The Rapture.*[3]

The word *rapture* comes from the Latin verb, *rapere,* which is used in the *Vulgate Bible* to translate the Greek, *harpadzo,* and literally means *to snatch away or catch up.*

For pre-tribulation (pre-*trib)* evangelicals, the classic rapture passage is found in 1 Thessalonians chapter 4. Paul the apostle wrote to the Thessalonians of the pleasant memories of days he spent with the infant body of believers in Thessalonica. He commends the body of believers for their faith, hope, love and perseverance in the face of persecution. Paul's efforts to guide the body of believers spiritually are visible through his affection toward them in his first letter that he sent to the Thessalonians.

Paul encourages the believers in Thessalonica to excel in their newfound faith, to increase and abound in their love for one another and to all, to comfort each other and edify one another, to rejoice and give thanks always. Paul completes his first letter to the body of believers with instruction concerning the return of our Lord Jesus Christ. It is interesting what Paul asks this young body of believers. In 1 Thess.2:19 NIV, Paul asks them, "For what is our hope, or joy, or crown of rejoicing? Is it not even you in the presence of our Lord Jesus Christ at His coming?" Christ's return signifies hope and comfort for those believers who are alive and those who have died. One of the most debated and often written about passages in the Bible with regard to the rapture is 1 Thess. 4:13-18.

This particular passage of scripture, when taken at face value, would appear to be self-explanatory. Paul is saying to the body of believers, "According to the Lord's own word, we tell you that we who are still alive, who are left till the coming of the Lord, will certainly not precede those who have fallen asleep". Paul was trying to comfort the church at Thessalonica because they had been worried about those believers who had already died. "For the Lord Himself will descend from heaven with a shout, with the voice of an archangel, and with the trumpet of God. And the dead in Christ will rise first." He will resurrect those who have died "in Christ", then both the dead and living body of believers "shall be caught up together in the clouds to meet the Lord in the air." Paul's final instruction to the Thessalonians was "therefore encourage each other with these words" (1 Thess. 4:13-18 NIV). In other words, Paul was giving them hope and comfort of the return of our Lord Jesus Christ.

Paul continues to give the Thessalonians instruction with regard to the timing of the coming of the Lord in 1 Thess. 5:1-3. He is concerned that the Thessalonians are aware that the Lord's return is like a *thief at night.* In 1 Cor. 1:7, the body of believers is urged to watch for Christ's return. (cf. Phil. 3:20-21).

Believers, both living and those who have died in Christ, will meet the Lord in midair and ascend to heaven. This body of believers will be transformed in their new bodies, they will appear before the judgment seat of Christ for their reward (1 Cor. 3:10-15). Paul reminds the body of believers that through "The grace of God which was given to me, as a wise builder I have laid the foundation, and another builds on it." Paul is referring to the foundation of Jesus Christ. Remember, that in the first epistle of Paul the apostle to the Corinthians, he shares words of counsel in answer to questions raised by the Corinthian believers. Paul further exhorts that "Each one take heed how he builds on it."

Because as Paul explains to the Corinthian believers, "Each one's work will become clear; for the Day will declare it, because it will be revealed by fire; and the fire will test each one's work, of what sort it is."

The body of believers as Christ's bride will enjoy the marriage supper of the Lamb (Rev. 19:5-9). The bride of Christ, the body of believers, will be dressed in fine linen. This fine linen is a symbol of holiness. The Levites, worship leaders of the temple, wore fine linen.

The main artery leading to the heart of the rapture issue is which school of thought will turn out to be true:

- ***Pre-Tribulation Rapture***—occurring ***before*** the Tribulation period begins.
- ***Mid-Tribulation Rapture***—occurring ***in the middle*** of the Tribulation period.
- ***Post-Tribulation Rapture***—occurring ***at the end*** of Daniel's 70th Week.
- ***Pre-Wrath Rapture***—occurring ***sometime in the last half*** of Daniel's 70th Week.

Revelation's seven seals, trumpets and bowl judgments will be visited upon the earth during this seven year period. Judgments ranging from the sun turning dark to a plague of painful boils occur during these dreadful seven years. Scripture teaches that a third of the earth will be destroyed during this seven year period and that people will still refuse to accept Jesus Christ as personal Lord and Savior and turn to God (Rev. 9:20-21). Non-believers will join the efforts of the Antichrist to gather against God and battle the Lord at Armageddon (Rev. 16:12-16). It is at the end of this great battle that God will defeat His enemies and set the stage for the final judgment. Details regarding the timing and sequence of events are still being hotly debated and will continue to be while there is a body of believers here on this earth.

Adherents of each of these positions typically cite 1 Cor. 15:51-53; 1 Thess. 4:14-17, Matt. 24:36-41, and John 14:2, yet with greatly differing reasons. Each group makes the assertion that anyone holding a different view must then be a poor scholar or simply ignorant of good biblical interpretation.

A high percentage of believers writing on the end-times have been a part of, or have been heavily influenced by, the pre-tribulation thinking of Dallas Theological Seminary scholars. "John F. Walvoord is one of the preeminent prophesy scholars and was Chancellor of Dallas Theological Seminary and on the school's faculty for over fifty years."[4] Hal Lindsay, Tim LaHaye, Robert Thomas, Thomas Ice, Timothy Demy, Mark Hitchcock, and Grant Jeffrey all teach an end-times sequence patterned substantially after Walvoord's teachings.

My personal belief is in a pre-tribulation rapture based upon studies of the Greek, Hebrew, and English scriptures. The other positions as shown below contain too many weak scripture connections to validate them.

Common Features of the *Rapture*

Features common to all rapture positions include:

- Jesus will come down from heaven, accompanied by archangels.
- A loud command will be issued.
- The trumpet call of God will sound.
- The dead in Christ rise first.
- Remaining believers will be changed and caught up.
- Jesus will ***meet in the air*** all those caught up.
- It will occur before the beginning of the Millennium.

Pre-Tribulation *Rapture*

Supporters of this position believe strongly in an early snatching away of born-again Christians from the earth. In this view, the *rapture* will come prior to the creation of a seven-year peace treaty between

Israel and a world ruler. This world ruler will later be revealed as the Antichrist.

Jesus revealed that the *rapture* would come, when most unexpected. "No one knows about that day or hour, not even the angels in heaven, nor the Son, but only the Father" (Matt. 24:36).

Critics of the pre-tribulation (*pre-trib*) position accuse adherents of adopting a position that is not ancient, citing visions experienced in 1830 by Margaret MacDonald, a 15 year old Scottish girl, which included a secret rapture of believers prior to the appearance of the Antichrist. Later, John Darby incorporated the essence of those visions into the doctrine he taught in America in his Christian community at Zion, Illinois.

Marvin Rosenthal says in his book, *The Pre-wrath Rapture of the Church*, that the *pre-trib* rapture "Can be traced back to John Darby and the Plymouth Brethren in the year 1830."[5] He does modify his strong assertion later in the book when he says, "Some scholars, seeking to prove error by association, have attempted (perhaps unfairly) to trace its origin back two years earlier to a charismatic, visionary woman named Margaret MacDonald."[6]

Adherents point out that there is ample evidence of church fathers validating the pre-tribulation position. Thomas Ice, in a refutation of the anti-pre-tribulation position says:

> Posttribulationists (*post-tribers*) often contend that the *pre-trib* position is built merely built upon an assumption that certain verses 'make sense' if and only if the *pre-trib* model of the rapture is assumed to be correct. However, they often fail to make it clear to their readers that they are just as dependent upon assumptions as they say *pre-tribers* are. Their error stems from failure to observe actual biblical distinctions.[7]

Non-pretribulationists sense that if the New Testament teaches immanency, then pre-tribulation rapture is virtually assured.[8]

Unlike *mid*—and *post-trib* supporters, *pre-trib* adherents differentiate between the various trumpets mentioned in passages about the last days (1 Cor. 15:52 and Rev. 11:15). The assumption is that the seventh trumpet is the last of the seven trumpets, a conclusion reasonable enough on the surface, but not explicit in scripture, thus failing the literal test.

Mid-Tribulation *Rapture*

Proponents of this position (aka. *mid-tribers*) believe strongly that Christians will endure at least half of the Tribulation Period, but will be caught up before the really bad events of the last half (Great Tribulation) begin.

Based upon a decision to understand Daniel's 70th Week as not actually getting serious until the Antichrist defiles the Temple in the middle of the Week, *mid-tribers* could consider themselves as *pre-tribers.* However, this is an intellectual stretch given the prophesied seven-year length of the period.

People holding this position tend to deny the doctrine of the immanent return of Christ.[9] Imminent means something that may happen any time, but not yet. There is both uncertainty as to timing and certainty as to occurrence of the happening. For *mid-tribers*, specific events must take place prior to Christ's rapture of believers:

- Entry into a treaty between Israel and a world ruler (Dan. 9:27).
- Rebuilding of the Temple in Jerusalem (Dan. 9:27—that may be defiled by the "ruler that will come.").
- Beginning of birth pains (Matt. 24:8).

Post-Tribulation *Rapture*

Defenders of this position believe strongly that Christians will go through the entire Tribulation Period with many supernaturally protected by the Lord and others martyred for their faith.

By equating the *seventh trumpet* (Rev. 11:15) with the *last trumpet* (1 Cor. 15:52), and citing the *trumpet call* mentioned in 1 Thess. 4:16 as support, *post-trib* advocates justify their position for a rapture of the church at the end of the Tribulation Period. In their view; all trumpets mentioned in end-times scriptures are equal.

A problem with this view is reconciling a *post-trib* position with Paul's statement in 1 Thess. 1:10b: ". . . Jesus, *who **rescues us from** the coming wrath.*" [Italics mine] *Rescues . . . from* is a good translation from the Greek, *roumenon . . . ek . . .*

Roumenon means to bring someone out of severe and acute danger. *Ek* means to move away from a place or situation. The actor in this process is Jesus, hence the clear understanding that believers will not go through any part of the Tribulation Period which is fraught with danger: both earthly ***and*** cosmic. The danger is associated with God's wrath manifested in judgment of unbelievers.

Pre-Wrath *Rapture*

Robert Van Kampen developed in the 1990s what is known today as the *Pre-Wrath* rapture position.[10] Like those who hold to a *mid-trib* position, supporters of this view believe that sometime during the last half of the Tribulation, but before the really bad part of the Great Tribulation begins, believers will be raptured, and thus avoid the trials promised to those who go through the entire 70th week. Adherents of a *Pre-Wrath* rapture position (*pre-wrathers*) believe, as do *mid-tribers*, that the first half of the seven-year tribulation as spoken of in Matt. 24:8 as the "beginning of birth pains." Both groups also believe that the last half is the really terrible Great Tribulation in which the people of the world and the earth itself will experience the fullness of God's wrath.

Imminence

Imminence is defined as something "liable to happen" or happen soon [11]; something impending ("about to happen").[12]

Christian believers have been expecting the imminent return of Christ since His resurrection.

The *Dictionary of Biblical Prophecy and End Times* states:

> Advocates of the pretribulation perspective hold that some of the passages (John 14:1-14; Rom. 13:11-12; 1 Cor. 7:29-31; 15:51-58; 1 Thess. 4:13-18) refer to the rapture (the secret coming of Christ to snatch his church away to heaven before the arrival of the Great Tribulation). The other texts refer to the second coming of Christ in visible power and glory after the Great Tribulation. Therefore, because the sign of the Great Tribulation pertains to Jesus' second coming and not the rapture, the latter can happen at any moment.
>
> Posttribulationists (those who equate the rapture with the second coming, placing it after the Great Tribulation) believe the signs of the times began at the first coming of Christ and will intensify before his return. Therefore, since these signs have already been set in motion, the second coming can occur at any time and is thus imminent.[13]

This highlights the problem sincere believers have with the *rapture*; its timing and manner of occurrence.

As for me, I believe with other pre-tribulationists that, unlike the second coming of Christ, there is nothing left to take place that would be necessary to the *rapture* happening and that the *rapture* could take place at any time.

Second Coming

The second coming, unlike the *rapture*, has a number of events that will precede it. See Chapter 21 for more discussion. The characteristics of the *rapture* and the *second coming* are clearly different.

Left Behind series

The popular *Left Behind* series of novels by Tim LaHaye and Jerry Jenkins stirred up much discussion and some animus among Christians. It has also affected non-believers by opening up opportunities to reflect on and discuss the place of Bible prophecy in relation to the world today. A *Newsweek* blog on The Daily Beast by David Gates opined:

> Readers identify with the *Left Behind* characters in part because they seldom speak in Christian clichés: as Jenkins says, starting out with the Rapture means "Anybody who would use evangelical lingo is gone after the first chapter of the first book." More important, Jenkins uses such characters as Rayford Steele's daughter Chloe to voice his own wrestlings with his faith. "To me there's a value in questioning, and even doubting sometimes. Chloe's big deal is how does this sound like a loving God? People disappear, planes crash, people die—even people who might have believed, but it's too late. There is indication in the prophecies that God will harden some people's hearts. I don't get it myself; I don't understand how that fits in with God's plan. Yeah, those are hard things." Jenkins is nearly as troubled as his critics by the apparently vengeful elements in the books, such as that episode in "Glorious Appearing" in which too-late penitents are sent to hell vainly bleating, "Jesus is Lord." "One of the toughest things I deal with is that there are some evangelicals, with familiar faces, who seem to like that part of it. You know, 'We're right, you're wrong, that's what the Bible says, someday you're going to kneel and admit it.' That should break our hearts."[14]

Gates closed with remarks by LaHaye and Jenkins about the timing and net effect of the rapture:

> Still, Jenkins knows that is what the Bible says, at least as he and LaHaye read it, and "we sort of have a responsibility

> to tell what it seems to say to us." For them—just as for Christians who think LaHaye and Jenkins have it all wrong—this is ultimately about love, for God and for their fellow humans. As they see it, they're on a rescue mission, with time running out. "We don't know when the Lord's going to come," LaHaye admits, and he likes to quote Matt. 24:35: "Of that day and hour no one knows, no, not even the angels of heaven, but My Father only." But don't the signs seem to be coming thick and fast? Even for evangelical Christians, of course, LaHaye and Jenkins's uncompromising reading of Scripture and of current events isn't the only choice. But if you assume, with them, that it's all true, the end won't be pretty for those left behind. While for those who listen up in time, it'll be a whole other story.[15]

Both LaHaye and Jenkins are firmly pre-tribulational in their view of the *rapture* timing. The 12-book original *Left Behind* series and the 4-book prequel series—sub-titled *Countdown to the Rapture*—was wildly popular, and widely read by both Christians and non-believers, giving an indication of the attraction of the topic of rapture.

Timing of a Pretribulation *Rapture*

If one allows for a pretribulation rapture, when will it take place? As LaHaye reminded us in the quote above, Matthew 24:36 (NIV) clearly states that, "No one knows about that day or hour, not even the angels in heaven, nor the Son, but only the Father." Jesus simply told us that life would be going on pretty much as it always has with: eating and drinking, marrying and giving in marriage. That time would simply arrive and surprise everyone when they least expected it.

Some pretribulation scholars place the *rapture* ***exactly*** at the beginning of the tribulation, others place it ***before*** (up to 3½ years*)* the peace covenant, which launches the tribulation. The expectation is that chaos resulting from the surprise departure of so many people will create a global environment conducive to wars (e.g. War of Gog and Magog) because the restraining influence of Christian leaders will be absent.

Some opponents of *pretribulation rapture* have styled this view as a *secret rapture*. My view is that it is not so secret, given the announcement by a trumpet call, but rather simply a *surprise*. Unless the trumpet call was heard only by believers who were attuned to it, the result of the disappearance of so many people with the concurrent chaos would preclude it being a secret. The mystery Paul revealed to believers in Corinth was of an instantaneous change which will take place concurrent with the raising of the dead at a trumpet call. Such an event will not likely pass unnoticed (1 Cor. 15:51-52).

Jesus told the disciples that one of two coworkers would disappear while at work (Matt. 24:40-41). I don't know about you, but if I was at work, possibly chatting about yesterday's Boise State University football scores, our boss, or family matters, and my coworker disappeared from my side, I think I would know it. It would ***not*** be a secret.

But God . . . !

CHAPTER 16

Coalition of Countries

> *[1] The word of the LORD came to me: [2] "Son of man, set your face against Gog, of the land of Magog, the chief prince of Meshech and Tubal; prophesy against him [3] and say: 'This is what the Sovereign LORD says: I am against you, O Gog, chief prince of Meshech and Tubal. [4] I will turn you around, put hooks in your jaws and bring you out with your whole army--your horses, your horsemen fully armed, and a great horde with large and small shields, all of them brandishing their swords. [5] Persia, Cush and Put will be with them, all with shields and helmets, [6] also Gomer with all its troops, and Beth Togarmah from the far north with all its troops--the many nations with you.* (Ezek. 38:1-6 NIV)

In Ezekiel chapters 38 and 39, the Bible lists specific nations, which will come against Israel in the last days in the War of Gog and Magog. Those people are currently forming a coalition of nation-states, which will comprise a major threat to Israel.

The cited nations include:

Magog

The land of Magog encompasses a region of Russia.

Meshech

Moscow is thought by many scholars to be the biblical Meshech.

Tubal

The part of Siberia through which the Tobolsk River flows is considered a strong candidate for the biblical Tubal.

Persia

Up until 1935, the country we now call Iran was called Persia.

Cush

In ancient times the geographic region called Cush included the modern lands of Ethiopia, part of the Sudan, and Eritrea.

Put

The geographic region now called Libya was formerly called Put.

Gomer

The Land of Gomer includes Turkey, possibly parts of the former East Germany, and portions of northern Europe occupied by the Gauls.

Beth Togarmah

Scholars speculate based on historical people movements that Beth Togarmah describes the area of modern day Turkey and Armenia.

"[M]any nations with you"

Though unnamed, one may safely assume that the "many nations" are those with a similar interest in attacking Israel for the purpose of obtaining her wealth and/or destroying her.

Most of these nations are descendants of Noah's son Japheth. One prominent exception is Cush who is descended from Noah's son Ham.

Concerns arise

In 2006, *Ynet News* published an article entitle, "Modern Day Gog and Magog," discussing the developments in the Middle East. In the article, reporter Ines Ehrlich stated that:

> Current world events are beginning to increasingly resemble the 2,500 year old Bible prophecy made by Ezekiel in chapters 38-39. Ezekiel foresaw the rise of Russia (or Turkey, depending on the interpretation) in a coalition with Iran and other Middle Eastern countries (Sudan, Ethiopia and Libya).[1]

Rabbis voiced worry on the occasion of the Israeli interception of a flotilla trying to break the naval blockade of Gaza in June 2010 and suggested that this might be the beginning of the war of Gog and Magog.[2]

In August 2011, Joel Rosenberg pondered Vladimir Putin's rise in Russia and whether or not he is the Gog of scripture, [3] citing Putin's:

- assertion that Americans are "parasite[s]" on global economy
- intention to create a merger with the tyrannical dictatorship of Belarus
- goal of creating a Eurasian Economic Union—likely with the Kremlin at the helm.

Rosenberg said, "Though Putin was, at that time, only the Prime Minister of Russia, he is on the rise and could become the Gog of Ezekiel's Gog and Magog."

The Economist reported that Putin's expected win in the March 2012 elections for President of Russia is at risk, given the:

> . . . Rigged election, a jailed popular blogger, an arrogant leader and quiescent television: in the past week the Kremlin has used all of these to trigger Russia's deepest political crisis in years. This may not be the beginning of a revolution, but it is the end of Vladimir Putin's era of alleged stability, which started over a decade ago.[4]

Putin has exhibited all of the signs of a Gog, as leader of Russia, but, as the world has seen, dictatorial leaders in 2011, have had a tough go, given the inclination of protestors to find the courage to speak and act out. As of this writing, Putin may not be the Gog of Ezekiel 38, but it is sure that someone will arise to fill that post at just the right time in God's plan.

With men of the ilk of Vladimir Putin in Russia, Mahmoud Ahmadinejad in Iran, and Bashar al-Assad in Syria, it is clear that God is setting up His plan for the prophesied war of Gog and Magog. These individual leaders may not be the final team to execute it, but alliances are forming which will.

It is interesting to consider the lineage of the peoples mentioned in Ezekiel related to Magog. Several of them are the names of the progeny of Noah's son Japheth (Gen. 10:1-5).

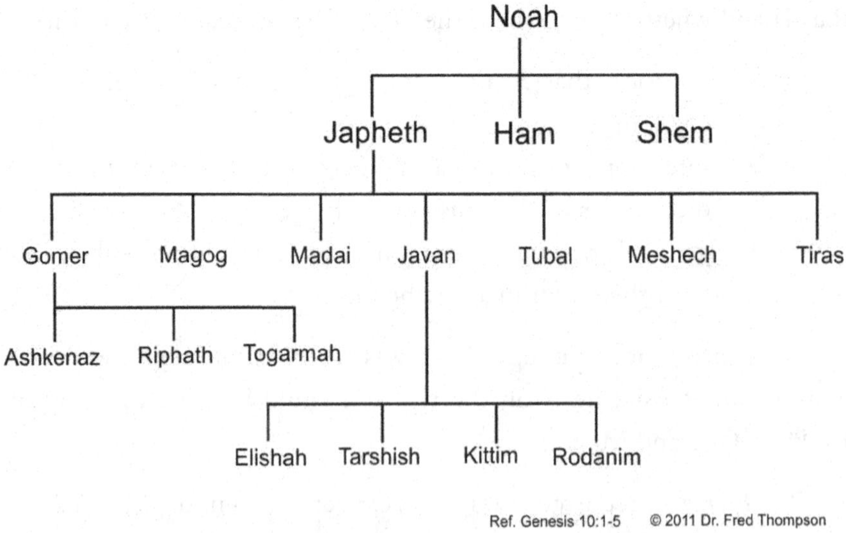

Note that Gomer, Magog, Tubal, Meshech, and [Beth] Togarmah are listed both as descendants and as partners in the coalition. These people groups come from the regions of the former Soviet Union, Eastern Europe, and Turkey. The remainder of the coalition members come from areas currently populated largely by followers of Mohammed—Libya, Ethiopia, the Sudan, and Iran. The *many nations with you* (Ezek. 38:6) are likely to include Syria, Lebanon, and some others currently unidentified.

Also intriguing is that the ancient people group called the Scythians formerly occupied the same region as the former Soviet Union countries of Kazakhstan, Kyrgyzstan, Tajikistan, Turkmenistan, and Uzbekistan. The progenitors of these races were widely known as fierce warriors; horsemen known and feared for their fighting ability. The Scythians are popularized as *Sith* warriors of the *Star Wars* movie series.

Russian leadership under Vladimir Putin is courting these countries for new partnerships in energy production and distribution.

When?

The next big question is—when will the war of Gog and Magog take place?

If the *rapture* takes place as expected by pre-tribulationists, the resultant world chaos could produce the opportunity for the Magog Coalition to attack Israel, a "land of unwalled villages . . . and a peaceful and unsuspecting people" (Ezek. 38:11 NIV).

Some end-times authors and scholars believe that the war of Gog and Magog could take place ***after*** the peace treaty is signed between Israel and the world ruler—Antichrist. If this is the timing, it needs to take place almost on top of the treaty signing to allow for the seven years of weapons left over to be consumed as fuel (Ezek. 39:9-10).

Careful reading of Revelation uncovers a reference to the "nations in the four corners of the earth—Gog and Magog" (Rev. 20:7-8), which leads some to interpret the War of Gog and Magog as taking place following the Millennium when Satan is released to again savage the earth just before his final incarceration in the lake of fire.

The problem with this timing is that there is no reference to the almost complete devastation of the armies involved, nor is there mention of:

- a great earthquake in the land of Israel (Ezek. 38:19)
- every man and beast trembling at God's presence (Ezek. 38:20)
- mountains overturned, cliffs crumbling, and walls falling down (Ezek. 38:20)
- every man's sword being against his brother (Ezek. 38:21)
- judgment executed with plague and bloodshed (Ezek. 38:22)
- torrents of rain, hailstones, and burning sulfur poured on Satan and his troops (Ezek. 38:22)
- God disarming the troops (Ezek. 39:3)
- troops dying on the mountains of Israel and being eaten by birds and wild animals (Ezek. 39:4)

Bottom Line

Ezekiel's prophecy ***will*** be fulfilled. I could be wrong about the war of Gog and Magog taking place after the pre-tribulation rapture, during the chaos before the seven-year Tribulation period begins. Some scholars place the war somewhere in the first half of the Tribulation, others during the second half (Great Tribulation).

The war as described in Ezekiel is unlikely to take place at the end of the Millennium for reasons stated above. But, know this—it ***will*** take place!

But God . . . !

CHAPTER 17

Vulture Population

> [4] *On the mountains of Israel you will fall, you and all your troops and the nations with you. I will give you as food to all kinds of carrion birds and to the wild animals.* (Ezek. 39:4 NIV)
>
> [17] *And I saw an angel standing in the sun, who cried in a loud voice to all the birds flying in midair, "Come, gather together for the great supper of God,* [18] *so that you may eat the flesh of kings, generals, and mighty men, of horses and their riders, and the flesh of all people, free and slave, small and great."* (Rev. 19:17-18 NIV)

Two wars (e.g. Gog & Magog and Armageddon) in Israel will result in so many dead that normal methods of burial, cremation, etc. will be inadequate to handle the casualties. Scripture states that on both occasions, God will have birds of the air complete the work required (Ezek. 39:4 and Rev. 19:17-18). The formerly endangered species list includes the Griffin vulture whose population had diminished to dangerous levels.

The Griffin vulture (*Gyps fulvus*) is of the species classified as Old World vultures, which belong to the family *Accipitridae*, which also includes eagles, buzzards, kites, and hawks.[1] Eagles and vultures are among those birds forbidden to be eaten by kosher Jews. (Lev. 11:13-19) This may be attributed to the fact that they consume carrion and thus are defiled.

Bible translators often translate the Hebrew *nesher* as *eagle* when it typically means *Griffin vulture*, which is the prevalent vulture species in Israel. Likewise the Greek *aetos* is translated as *eagle* in the New Testament.

In 2004, Dr. Noah Hutchings was quoted in an article entitled, "Flesh-Eating Birds Gather in Israel":

> The buzzards of Israel are displaying affection for each other in multiplying and also, the Israeli people have a rather strange affection for the buzzards . . . The birds of prey are frequently poisoned by Israeli farmers. Israel's 'Spreading Wings' program to resuscitate the vulture population has set up 20 feeding and nesting stations around the country.
>
> When the Jews were absent from the land during the Diaspora, the land became a virtual desert. With no trees or grain crops, the wild animal and bird population of Israel, including the vultures, disappeared. Now that Israel is back, trees cover the land and extensive farming of all kinds provides food for the birds and wild animals once more. The vulture population at Gamla on the east side of the Sea of Galilee has been increasing in recent years, but pesticides and eating deer and other animals which have been shot has also poisoned some vultures.
>
> But, setting up nesting and feeding stations for vultures throughout Israel is increasing the vulture population. Now, even mating vultures that have been injured and cannot fly

> are mating because of the scientific effort which has made this type of mating possible. Why does Israel have such an affinity for vultures? Prophetic Scriptures assign a very important function to the fowls of the air who feast primarily on carrion, like vultures, after Jesus has slaughtered untold millions of the army of Antichrist.[2]

In 2009, while visiting Israel, our tour guide shared with the group that the Griffin vulture population has been reported to be on the increase. Our tour group went to the Golan Heights at the site called Gamla, overlooking the Galilee and saw flights of the birds over the valley below.

Since that time, the population has declined again because of farmers poisoning dead livestock to discourage wolves and jackals which ravage their herds. When the vultures eat the poisoned carrion, they and their young die. In 2011, Israeli conservation groups have appealed to other nations to help with the problem:

> Protecting Israel's endangered scavenger birds, especially the majestic Griffon vulture, will be the main agenda item at an international conference in Tel Aviv next week being organized by The Society for the Protection of Nature in Israel and the Israel Nature and Parks Authority. The Israel Electric Corporation is also providing assistance.
>
> "Every bird has something special, and with vultures, it is the noble way they soar," said Dan Alon, of the *Society for the Protection of Nature in Israel* (SPNI's) Israel Ornithology Center.
>
> Alon has been working for more than a decade to assist various bodies in saving Israel's vultures. But recently he and his colleagues have become concerned that the decline in the vulture population will soon become irreversible,

> and so they have organized the conference, to take place at Tel Aviv University.
>
> "I remember the days we would see dozens of vultures soaring right at eye level at the cliffs of the Gamla reserve. Today you hardly see any," Alon said.
>
> According to figures of the Israel Nature and Parks Authority, less than 40 nesting pairs of Griffon vultures are left in Israel, as opposed to nearly 1,000 before the establishment of the state.[3]

Technological advances also play a part in the reduction of the Griffin vulture population. The growing use of wind generators kills the birds when they try to fly through them to their regular feeding grounds. Un-insulated electrical transmission wires contribute to the death of the birds as well.

Despite the efforts of the Jerusalem Zoo and conservation groups to regenerate the population, success has not yet been achieved. These groups run centers for incubating the bird eggs and release the hatched birds into the wild when ready.

First reports about the increase of the Griffin vulture population seemed to signal the possibility that these birds would at some early time play their role in the prophesied bird banquets. Now, it appears that time will be needed for the vulture population to grow sufficiently to accomplish the large task of assisting with the dispatch of the dead bodies produced by the two great battles of the end-times (Ezek. 39:4 and Rev. 19:17-18).

It appears that the voraciousness of the wolves and jackals will also be ready to perform their roles when God is ready for this phase of the end-times. Wolves have even learned to climb the high fences erected to protect farmer's livestock herds.[4]

But God . . . !

CHAPTER 18

Third Temple in Jerusalem

> [1] *I was given a reed like a measuring rod and was told, "Go and measure the temple of God and the altar, and count the worshipers there.* [2] *But exclude the outer court; do not measure it, because it has been given to the Gentiles. They will trample on the holy city for 42 months.* (Rev. 11:1-2 NIV)

Both Jewish and Christian believers have expressed their passionate desire to see the Temple in Jerusalem rebuilt. Jews are preparing right now to begin construction on the Temple. Furniture and worship implements have already been fabricated with few exceptions from descriptions and plans found in scripture.

John was told in Revelation 11:1-2 to "Measure the temple," excluding the outer court of the Gentiles which will be trampled by the Gentiles for 3½ years. This could not happen unless the 3rd Temple was built on the Temple Mount. Given the current presence of Muslim holy sites in that location, something would have to be done to remove the Dome of the Rock and the Al Aqsa Mosque from the Temple Mount before the 3rd Temple could be built. Logically, this is what would have to happen: Dome of the Rock and the Al Aqsa Mosque would have to be destroyed or dismantled to make room for the Jewish Temple.

The bottom line is that for a temple to be measured and for the Antichrist to be able to defile it at the mid-point of the Tribulation, an actual temple must exist prior to that. Because the 2nd Temple, built by Zerubbabel following the Babylonian captivity of the Jews from 606 to 537 B.C. and renovated by King Herod around 19 B.C., was destroyed by the Romans in 70 A.D., nothing remains of it on the Temple Mount in 2011.

Another surprise found in scripture is God's promise to restore the Temple treasures from Babylon, when it was time to rebuild the 2nd Temple. Many were removed again by the Romans in 70 A.D. (cf. Jer. 27:21-22).

Rosenberg reports in *Epicenter*:

> Likewise, the prophet Isaiah promised the children of Israel that the First Temple treasures would be restored to them when it was time to build the Second Temple. In Isaiah 52:11, instructing the Israelites to return from their captivity in Babylon, the prophet wrote, "Purify yourselves, you who carry home the sacred objects of the LORD." . . . . Do such verses, as well as others found in the books of Nehemiah and Ezra, provide a precedent that God is safeguarding the Second Temple's treasures for the children of Israel and will reveal them when it is time to build the Third Temple? Some Jewish and Christian scholars think so. We simply do not know for sure. But the notion is tantalizing. [1]

During a visit to Israel, my wife and I were able to see a full-size replica of a 24 ct. golden menorah on display in the Old City of Jerusalem. The organization known as the Temple Institute has taken on the task of creating all of the furniture and peripheral tools and equipment necessary to resume sacrifices in the new Temple. To date they have created over 90 items for that purpose.

Assumption of Rebuilding

The Temple Institute web site states:

> The Temple Mount, in Hebrew *Har Habayit*, known in the Torah as Mount Moriah, is the holiest spot in the world for all mankind. It is the location of both the First and Second Holy Temple.
>
> Here, G-d commanded Abraham, father of the Jewish people, to bind his son Isaac. According to all the prophets of Israel, when the Third Temple is rebuilt on this same spot, this will usher in an era of peace and universal harmony unparalleled in the history of mankind. It is a fundamental principle of Jewish faith that the Temple will be rebuilt. [2]

Controversy

Given that the Temple Mount (*Al-Haram Al-Sharif* for Muslims) is a hotly-contested property, much will need to change before Jews may find the freedom to build the Third Temple on the historic Mount Moriah location.

Al Haram Al Sharif is currently the home of the Muslim Dome of the Rock, allegedly the location where Mohammed rose up on his horse into heaven to meet Allah, and the Al Aqsa Mosque where thousands of Muslims worship. Given the state of Jewish-Moslem relations today, it is highly unlikely that the Moslem *Wakf*, currently the custodian of that real estate by agreement with the Israeli government, will allow the building of a new Jewish Temple.

Some Israeli scholars have suggested that a compromise might be possible, placing the new Temple in the space ***between*** the Dome of the Rock and the Al Aqsa Mosque. Scholars are not in agreement about the exact location of the original Holy of Holies which would determine the correct location of the temple building.

With the exception of Jerome, translator of the scriptures into the Latin (the Vulgate version of the Bible), most other early Christian theologians (e.g. Irenaeus, Tertullian, and Cyril—Bishop of Jerusalem) believed that the Antichrist would rebuild the Third Temple in Jerusalem. Hippolytus (A.D. 170-236), Bishop of Rome, for example, drew parallels between the reality of Christ and the imitative behavior of the Antichrist. In his *Treatise on Christ and Antichrist*, Hippolytus said, "The Savior raised up and showed His holy flesh like a temple, and he [Antichrist] will raise up a temple of stone in Jerusalem." [3]

Other prophecy teachers simply believe that, after the Antichrist appears as a somewhat peaceful world ruler and enters into a seven-year treaty with Israel, the way will be clear for Jews to build the Third Temple.

But God . . . !

CHAPTER 19

False Messiahs

> [24] *For false Christs and false prophets will appear and perform great signs and miracles to deceive even the elect—if that were possible.*
>
> (Matt. 24:24 NIV)

While false messiahs have emerged throughout recorded history, today, there appears to be more individuals who claim to fill that role. For example, Islam looks forward to the coming return of their Mahdi (the 12th Imam) to fill the role.

Messiah/Christ

Messiah, from the Hebrew mashiyach, means *anointed one*. The equivalent in Greek is Christos, which also means *anointed one*. *Anointed one* signifies one who has been appointed to a purpose.

In fact, *Messiah*, *Christ*, and *Anointed One* always refer to Jesus in both the old and new testaments. Messiah, Christ, and Anointed One are synonymous and may be used interchangeably.

False messiahs/christs

Jesus warned that many would appear in His name at the end of the age, claiming to be the Christ and also perform signs and miracles that could deceive even true believers. (Matt. 24:4-5, 24)

Over the ages

19th Century

- John Nichols Thom (1799-1838)—"Claimed to be the 'saviour of the world' and the reincarnation of Jesus Christ and his body temple of the Holy Ghost."
- Arnold Potter (1804-1872)—a Schismatic Latter Day Saint leader who "Claimed the spirit of Jesus Christ entered into his body and he became 'Potter Christ' Son of the living God."
- Bahá'u'lláh (1817-1892)—"Claimed to be the prophesized fulfillment and Promised One of all the major religions;" founded the Baha'i Faith movement.
- William W. Davies (1833-1906)—another Schismatic Latter Day Saint leader "Declared that [his son, Arthur] was the reincarnated Jesus Christ."
- Mirza Ghulam Ahmad of Qadian, India (1835-1908)—"Claimed to be the awaited Mahdi as well as (Second Coming) and likeness of Jesus the promised Messiah at the end of time."

20th Century

- Haile Selassie I (1892-1975)—the Rastafari movement claimed he was the promised Messiah.
- George Ernest Roux (1903-1981)—founder of the Universal Christian Church, claimed to be Jesus and later, God.
- Ernest Norman (1904-1971)—claimed to be Jesus in a past life.

- Sun Myung Moon (1920-)—"Believed by members of the Unification Church to be the Messiah."
- Jim Jones (1931-1978)—founded the Peoples Temple and "Claimed to be the reincarnation of Jesus, Akhenaten, Buddha, Vladimir Lenin, and Father Divine in the 1970s."
- Marshall Applewhite (1931-1997)—"Founded the Heaven's Gate cult" and declared, "I, Jesus—Son of God," announcing the end of the world with the arrival of the Hale-Bopp comet in 1997.
- Laszlo Toth (1940-)—"Hungarian-born Australian who claimed he was Jesus Christ as he vandalized Michelangelo's Pietà with a geologist hammer in 1972."
- José Luis de Jesús Miranda (1946-)—"Puerto Rican founder, leader and organizer of Growing in Grace based in Miami, Florida, who claims that the resurrected Christ "integrated himself within me" in 2007."
- Inri Cristo (1948-)—"a Brazilian astrologer who claims to be the second Jesus reincarnated in 1969."
- Shoko Asahara (1955-)—founded the controversial Japanese religious group Aum Shinrikyo in 1984. He declared himself 'Christ', Japan's only fully enlightened master and the "Lamb of God."
- David Koresh (1959-1993)—"born Vernon Wayne Howell, was the leader of a Branch Davidian religious sect in Waco, Texas, though never directly claiming to be Jesus himself, proclaimed that he was the final prophet and "the Son of God, the Lamb" in 1983."

21th Century

- David Shayler (1965-)—"In the summer of 2007, former [British] MI5 agent and whistleblower proclaimed himself to be the Messiah."

- Oscar Ramiro Ortega-Hernandez (1990-)—"In November of 2011 Mr. Ortega-Hernandez shot 9 rounds from a knock-off AK-47 at the White House in Washington D.C. believing that he is Jesus Christ sent to kill President Obama because President Obama is the anti-Christ."[1]

On the whole, these people are deceived themselves, if not simply mentally challenged. None of them are reported to have produced the signs and miracles Jesus warned about and thus may be dismissed out of hand.

Just because someone proclaims that what they say is true or even gets their statement published does not make it true.

When the end times that Jesus spoke about are truly in motion, the world may expect to see and hear of signs and miracles that seem real and are able to hoodwink everyone. Some may be real.

Whether the signs and wonders are real or counterfeit may be decided by referring to: "The *signs he was given* power to do" (Rev. 13:13-14). [Italics mine] This phrase indicates that God gives power to a certain individual—the False Prophet—to perform actual miracles under the auspices of the Antichrist for His (God's) last-days purpose.

Counterfeit signs and wonders may be, and have been, performed by the false messiahs present in the world throughout history.

Christian believers must at all times walk close to the Lord and discern the source of falsehood through the agency of the Holy Spirit. (1 John 4:1-5) Those who become believers during the Tribulation must be especially vigilant and discerning regarding signs, wonders and miracles.

But God . . . !

CHAPTER 20

Seven Years of Tribulation

> [26] *After the sixty-two 'sevens,' the Anointed One will be cut off and will have nothing. The people of the ruler who will come will destroy the city and the sanctuary. The end will come like a flood: War will continue until the end, and desolations have been decreed.* [27] *He will confirm a covenant with many for one 'seven.' In the middle of the 'seven' he will put an end to sacrifice and offering. And on a wing of the temple he will set up an abomination that causes desolation, until the end that is decreed is poured out on him.* (Dan 9:26-27 NIV)

Daniel prophesied that there would be a week of years (i.e. Daniel's *Seventieth Week*) of increasing trouble in the world. Revelation likewise goes into great detail about events, which will take place during those seven years. Some events occurring today are clear precursors to or foreshadowing of events prophesied in scripture for that period.

Trouble among humanity has been a part of life throughout recorded history. Yet today, trouble seems to be coming from all quarters and especially directed toward God's chosen people, the Jews.

Certainly "wars and rumors of wars" have been a fairly constant challenge. Matthew's Gospel warns of such things as a precursor to the end times. (Matt. 24:6) In order to allow these events to *break out of the pack*, one must consider the juxtaposition of other prophesied events:

- Nation will rise against nation.
- Kingdoms will rise against kingdom.
- There will be famines and earthquakes in various places.
- Believers will be handed over to be persecuted.
- Jews will be hated by all nations.
- Apostasy will occur.
- Former believers will betray and hate Christians.
- Many false prophets will deceive people.
- Wickedness will increase.
- The love of many (former believers) growing cold.
- The gospel will be preached ***in*** all the earth.
- The Temple will be the site of an abomination of desolation.

From reading or listening to printed or broadcast news and learning of events from Internet articles, RSS feeds and such, it seems that we may already be at the threshold of the Tribulation period. Some think it may have started several years ago. See Chapter 15 for a discussion of the timing of the *great snatching away* (aka *rapture*). Depending on which rapture position a person holds, the tribulation will affect people differently. Believers who embrace a pre-tribulation rapture view, will, by definition, have no part in the Tribulation.

Fire the starting gun

One cardinal event has not yet taken place which will signal the start of the Tribulation—the signing of a seven-year peace treaty between Israel and a ruler representing the entire world. (Dan. 9:27)

John's Apocalypse

Walvoord's *Revelation* says, "Taking into account all the relevant evidence, both internal and external, the strongest view [of the time of writing] is that the apostle John wrote the book of Revelation in the year A.D. 95 while exiled by the Roman emperor Domitian to the island of Patmos."[1]

The book of Revelation (i.e. Apocalypse) starts off with a description of the apostle John's incarceration on the island of Patmos in Greece, then moves on into his visionary experience with the Son of Man (Jesus), and into letters written to seven churches in Asia Minor: Ephesus, Smyrna, Pergamum, Thyatira, Sardis, Philadelphia, and Laodicea (see Chapter 12). The next scene opens on a time of worship around the throne of God in heaven and introduction of the Lamb of God and His right to open a seven-sealed scroll. The Lamb of God, of course, is Jesus.

In reading Revelation, one must take care to avoid over-spiritualizing the text. Some of the descriptions of participants or events may ***seem*** to invite a metaphorical interpretation. It will be best to take what it says literally unless the text itself indicates a metaphorical interpretation is appropriate. One sign this may be true is use of the word "like" (e.g. in the sense of *similar, reminiscent of, comparable to,* etc.) in reference to the subject.

For example, the phrase, "The sun turned black like sackcloth made of goat hair" would be familiar to people living in the Middle East near nomadic Bedouins (Rev. 6:12b). Their tents were often woven of black goat hair. The passage clearly does not mean the sun would be woven, but rather that the color of black goat hair would characterize the sun's appearance.

As the Lamb opens the seals, we discover seven plague judgments unfolding. From their sequence and description, it appears that the seven Seal judgments enfold the seven Trumpet judgments and, in turn, the seven Bowl judgments.

Seals opened

The first four seals are described in secular and religious literature as the Four Horsemen of the Apocalypse. The last three seals are described simply as seals.

First seal (Rev. 6:1-2)

> One of the four living creatures (cf. Rev. 4:6b-9; Ezek. 1:4-22) invited John to come. A white horse with a rider, who held a bow, was given a crown, and went out "conquering and to conquer."

Second seal (Rev. 6:3-4)

> A second living creature invited John again to come. A fiery red horse carried a rider with a large sword. The rider had been given power to take peace from the earth and make men kill one another.

Third seal (Rev. 6:5-6)

> The third living creature said, "Come." A black horse whose rider was carrying a set of weighing scales appeared. The scales evidently were used for commerce, and not justice, as the text mentions measures of food stuffs.

Fourth seal (Rev. 6:7-8)

> The fourth living creature said, "Come." A pale horse, whose rider was named, "Death." Hades followed close

behind him. This rider was given power over one-fourth of the earth to kill by sword, famine and plague, and by the wild beasts of the earth.

Fifth seal (Rev. 6:9-11)

When the Lamb opened the seal, cries of martyrs situated under the heavenly altar were heard and they were given white robes and counseled to remain patient until all who would be martyred arrived.

Sixth seal (Rev. 6:12-17)

A great earthquake ensued as this seal was opened, the sun turned black and the moon turned red. Stars in the sky fell to the earth, the sky receded like a scroll, and mountains and islands moved from their place. The powerful, affluent and everyone else cried out for mercy out of abject fear asking the mountains to fall on them so they would be hidden from the face of the Lamb's wrath.

Seventh seal (Rev. 8:1-5)

After a brief ½ hour intermission, trumpets were issued to seven angels for the next phase.

144,000 sealed (Rev. 7:1-8)

After the sixth seal was opened, an angel came with the seal of the living God and placed it on the foreheads of 144,000 Jewish believers from each of the twelve tribes of Israel. From the tribes of:

- Judah 12,000
- Reuben 12,000
- Gad 12,000
- Asher 12,000
- Naphtali 12,000
- Manasseh 12,000

- Simeon 12,000
- Levi 12,000
- Issachar 12,000
- Zebulun 12,000
- Joseph 12,000
- Benjamin 12,000

The land, sea, or trees were not to be harmed until the sealing of the 144,000 was completed to mark them as protected.

Great multitude in white robes (Rev. 7:9-17)

A second great time of worship will take place around the throne in heaven among those martyred during the Tribulation.

Trumpet judgments

The seven angels who were issued trumpets got ready to sound them. Timothy Demy and Thomas Ice note that, "a trumpet was used in the ancient world to signal a special announcement or major event that was about to happen."[2] The events to follow certainly fulfill the definition of major events. Following the short, half-hour interlude accompanied by offerings of prayers and a resounding crescendo to the worship with peals of thunder, rumblings, flashes of lightning, and an earthquake, the trumpets began to sound. (Rev. 8:1-6)

Prophecy scholar Robert Thomas notes:

> In contradistinction to the last three trumpets, ***the first four afflict natural objects***, (i.e. earth, trees, grass, sea, rivers, and the like). ***The fifth and sixth have men as their special objects***, and unlike the first four which are connected and interdependent, are separate and independent. In contrast to these two, the first four have only an indirect effect on mankind. Besides these differences, the voice of the eagle in 8:13 separates the trumpets into two groups. [3] [Bolding and italicizing mine for emphasis]

First trumpet judgment (Rev. 8:7)

A third of the earth's vegetation is destroyed by hail, fire and blood.

Second trumpet judgment (Rev. 8:8-9)

A third of the sea life is destroyed by a large burning object, "like a great mountain," cast into the sea.

Third trumpet judgment (Rev. 8:10-11)

A third of the fresh water is poisoned by a great burning star which fell from the sky.

Fourth trumpet judgment (Rev. 8:12-13)

One third of the sun, moon and stars are darkened and the first woe is pronounced by an angel flying in mid-heaven.

Fifth trumpet judgment (Rev. 9:1-12)

Demonic locusts are released from the abysmal bottomless pit by a star which fell from heaven (Satan). These locusts are given power to sting and torment unsaved humans for five months.

Sixth trumpet judgment (Rev. 9:13-21)

Two hundred million demonic warriors riding demonic horses are released by four designated angels currently bound at the Euphrates River. The armies fought with plagues of fire, smoke and brimstone to kill one-third of unsaved humans using some really terrible horses of war to convey them around the earth.

Seventh trumpet judgment (Rev. 11:15-19)

This begins with a time of worship in heaven around the throne of God. More crescendo of activity takes place: flashes of lightning, rumblings, peals of thunder, an earthquake, and a great hailstorm. It includes all of the Bowl judgments.

Parenthetic activity

After the sixth trumpet and before the seventh trumpet sounds, several things happened:

- An angel opened a little scroll and introduced seven secret thunders (Rev. 10).
- Two witnesses appeared and prophesied for 1260 days, rejecting any attempts to remove them. When they finished their testimony, God allowed them to be killed, but brought them back to life after three days, whereupon they ascended to heaven in a cloud (Rev. 11:1-13).
- A woman, "clothed with the sun, with the moon under her feet, and a crown of twelve stars on her head" was found to be pregnant, delivered a man-child who was snatched up to God's throne, denying the dragon [Satan] his intended pleasure at destroying the child. The dragon was hurled to the earth along with his [evil] angels with him. Heaven then rejoiced. The dragon tried to pursue the woman, but failed because she was given wings like an eagle to escape to God's protection, frustrating the dragon no end (Rev. 12:1-13:1a).
- A beast from the sea appeared. He had ten horns and seven heads and crowns on the ten horns. His appearance was like a leopard, but with feet like a bear, and a mouth like a lion. The dragon [Satan] gave the beast his power and throne and great authority. The beast had been wounded on his head, but was healed. Men worshiped the dragon because of the beast. The beast was proud and blasphemous and exercised his authority for forty-

two months (1260 days). His authority was limitless and he persecuted believers and conquered them (Rev. 13:1b-10).

- A beast from the earth appeared at the mid-point of the *seven years* as the other beast's assistant. This beast had two horns like a lamb, but spoke like a dragon. He made all people worship the first beast and required everyone to take a mark to enable buying and selling. He was given power to perform miraculous signs, deceiving the earth's inhabitants. Those who declined to take the mark he had killed (Rev. 13:11-18).
- The Lamb (Jesus) stood on Mt. Zion and together with 144,000 sealed, blameless saints, sang a new song audible only to those who were sealed (Rev. 14:1-5).
- An angel proclaimed the gospel to the whole world. A second angel announced the demise of Babylon. And a third angel warned that anyone with the mark of the beast would drink of the fury of God. A voice from heaven blessed those who might die in the Lord from that point on (Rev. 14:6-13).
- Jesus then harvested the earth. An angel harvested the unrighteous and cast them into "the great winepress of God's wrath" (Rev. 14:14-20).

Bowl judgments

Following another time of rejoicing in heaven, seven angels with the final seven plagues (*bowls of God's wrath*) arrived (Rev. 16:1).

First bowl judgment (Rev. 16:2)

Ugly, painful sores break out on the bodies of people marked by and who worshipped the beast.

Second bowl judgment (Rev. 16:3)

Sea turned to blood, killing every living thing in it.

Third bowl judgment (Rev. 16:4-7)

All fresh waters turned to blood.

Fourth bowl judgment (Rev. 16:8-9)

Sun was given power to scorch people. They cursed God's name, but refused to repent.

Fifth bowl judgment (Rev. 16:10-11)

Kingdom of the beast was plunged into darkness. People again cursed God and still refused to repent.

Sixth bowl judgment (Rev. 16:12-16)

The great river Euphrates was dried up and a plague of frog demons performing miraculous signs and gathering the kings of the earth for the final battle on the great day of God Almighty. The kings were gathered together in the valley of Mt. Megiddo for the battle of Armageddon.

Seventh bowl judgment (Rev. 16:17-21)

The final announcement, "It is done," was made with flashes of lightning, peals of thunder, and a severe earthquake which split the city of Jerusalem into three parts. Cities throughout the world collapsed. Islands fled away and mountains were flattened. One-hundred-pound hailstones crushed men, yet they still cursed God.

Woman on the Beast (Rev. 17)

Spiritual Babylon was revealed to John by one of the seven angels with the bowls. She was called *Mystery Babylon the Great, Mother of Harlots, and of the Abominations of the Earth.* A thoroughly evil and nasty woman to whom, the nations of the earth have prostituted themselves spiritually, morally, and ethically. She is dripping with the blood of the righteous saints that died under her leadership and example.

The beast she rode came up out of the Abyss, empowered by Satan, using the Antichrist as a vessel, but ending up in eternal judgment. End-times scholar Robert Thomas provides additional insight into the beast:

> In explaining the beast, the angel uses several details from chapters 11 and 13 and adds new information: "The beast whom you saw was and is not, and is about to ascend out of the abyss, and he departs into perdition; and those who dwell upon the earth will marvel, whose names are not written upon the book of life from the foundation of the world, seeing the beast, that he was and is not and will be present". In each of his appearances in this book, the beast is either an empire or the ruler of that empire. Each head of the beast is a partial incarnation of satanic power that rules for a given period, so the beast can exist on earth without interruption in the form of seven consecutive kingdoms, but he can also be nonexistent at a given moment in the form of one of an empire's kings. The nonexistent beast in v. 8 must therefore be a temporarily absent king over the empire that will exist in the future.
>
> The designation of the beast as the one who "was and is not, and is about to ascend out of the abyss" ties him to the beast with the death-wound who was healed in 13:3, 12, 14. Both there and here the earth-dwellers express amazement . . . The words "is not" refer to the beast's death, and his ascent from the abyss means he will come to life again (cf. 13:14). This is the same as his reappearance as an eighth king in 17:11. His departure to perdition, "he departs into perdition," is his future assignment to the lake of fire (19:20).
>
> An understanding of the past-present-future description of the beast requires the establishing of a point of reference for the designation. When is "now," the point of the beast's

"not being"? One opinion is that it is the entirety of the present era, since the defeat of the beast by the Lamb at Calvary. This views the point of John's writing in the last decade of the first century as a natural understanding of the "now." It is a confusion of the beast with the dragon, however, if one takes 20:1-3 and the binding of Satan to be this "is-not" condition of the beast. Christ wounded the head of the serpent, not the beast, at Calvary. The beast cannot in any sense be in the abyss throughout this age so as to allow him to arise therefrom at the end of the age. In the form described in chapters 13 and 17, he had no existence before Calvary and will not exist until the future.

Another explanation for the "is-not" condition takes it as the recurring cycle of the waning of world conquests that are antagonistic to God. Nazi Germany and the Soviet Union are examples from the past. Yet this view coincides with an idealistic view of the Apocalypse and does not account for the details and events that connect this beast's activity with the return of Christ.

It is better to locate the "is-not" state of the beast entirely in the future and make that the point of reference for the total description. That state must coincide with the death wound of the beast in 13:3, 12, 14. This is his career midpoint, i.e., a time at the very beginning of chapter 13 when he comes up out of the sea. This is most probably a point at the very middle of the seventieth week, between the beast's human and superhuman careers. Whenever it is, it must have a relationship to the period just before Christ's return in order to be relevant to the last of the seven last plagues to which this intercalation attaches. How the reference point for "is-not" can differ from that in 17:10 where the sixth kingdom that "is" dates during John's lifetime is a legitimate question to raise. The answer lies in a literary difference between the two passages. Verse 8 is a part of the chapter that is purely prophetic, but vv. 9-11 is an injected explanation to help in understanding the prophecy. All these considerations lead to the conclusion that the perspective of this description of the beast is entirely future, at a point just before the beast from the sea begins his three and a half year reign. [4]

Fall of Commercial Babylon (Rev. 18)

John records the utter anguish of business enterprises, shippers, and the customers of the commercial and economic center called Babylon in its demise. The angel announces:

- the fall of Babylon and its new role as a home for demons and every evil spirit
- the anguish of those who enjoyed adulterous relationships with her
- a call for believers remaining in Babylon to depart
- a lament for rulers who relied on her largess to prosper
- global merchants weeping because they lost customers at her fall
- sea captains mourning at her fall for the loss of revenue shipping goods in and out of Babylon

An angel illustrated the downfall of Babylon symbolically with the casting of a large millstone into the sea and listed things that would no longer be a part of that city:

- the departure of musicians and merriment from the city
- the loss of work for employees
- the discovery of the deaths of righteous people there

Rejoicing and Worship in Heaven (Rev. 19)

After the many dark and terrible events that will take place during the Tribulation, there is a season of rejoicing and worship in heaven. Customarily, one might think that this book of John's Revelation is a mostly gloomy, dark, fear filled tome. However, alongside of the bad events are a number of occasions of joy, praise to God and worship:

- There is worship around the throne (Rev. 4).
- Lamb appears and is found worthy to open the scrolls accompanied by the singing of a new song in heaven (Rev. 5).
- Rejoicing among the martyred saints who died for their testimony (Rev. 7:9-17).
- Thanksgiving to God at the sounding of the seventh trumpet. (Rev. 11:15-18).
- Rejoicing in heaven as the dragon's (Satan's) intentions were thwarted (Rev. 12:10-12).
- Shouts of praise to God in heaven after the seventh bowl judgment was poured out and victory declared (Rev. 19:1-8).

As we Christians know, in the end we win, which provides opportunities for praise and worship.

Arrival of Jesus on a White Horse (Rev. 19:9-21)

Satan's servant, the Antichrist, arrived on a white horse at the beginning of the Tribulation, attempting to show his right to rule. But Jesus came at just the right time, also on a white horse, to settle the matter of who is really in charge in the universe.

But God . . . !

CHAPTER 21

Second Coming of Christ

> [8] *Listen! Your watchmen lift up their voices; together they shout for joy. When the LORD returns to Zion, they will see it with their own eyes.* (Isa. 52:8 NIV)
>
> [16] *"Therefore, this is what the LORD says: 'I will return to Jerusalem with mercy, and there my house will be rebuilt. And the measuring line will be stretched out over Jerusalem,' declares the LORD Almighty.* (Zech. 1:16 NIV)
>
> [4] *On that day his feet will stand on the Mount of Olives, east of Jerusalem, and the Mount of Olives will be split in two from east to west, forming a great valley, with half of the mountain moving north and half moving south.*
>
> (Zech. 1:16 NIV)

Increasingly, Christians are prayerfully yearning for the return of Jesus Christ prophesied in scripture. This event is one that many people look for. Stating the obvious, for there to be a second coming, there must have been a first coming.

At his first coming, Jesus:

- Was born of a virgin in a nondescript stable in Bethlehem (Luke 2:1-7).
- Listened and questioned the teachers in the temple at the age of twelve (Luke 2:41-50).
- Was baptized by John (3:21-22).
- Was tempted by the devil for 40 days in the desert (Matt. 4:1-11; John 4:1-13).
- Began his ministry at the age of thirty (John 2:1-11).
- Went on to teach and disciple his followers (Mark 3:13-19; John 1:35-51).
- Performed many miracles.

Near the end of his earthly ministry, Jesus taught His disciples about events to come (Matt. 24).

Jesus told His disciples:

- He was going on ahead of them to prepare a place for them (John 14:2).
- The world would not see him before long (speaking of His death), yet the disciples ***would*** see him (John 14:19).
- He will come back (John 14:28).
- At the end of the Tribulation period, Jesus' sign will appear in the sky and everyone on earth will see it (Matt. 24:29-30).

To understand the importance of Christ's return, J. Oliver Buswell says, "In the Second Coming of Christ, in the consummation of God's redemptive program, He will vindicate His creative purpose, and His image in man as vice-regent in the creation will be fully realized."[1]

Before He Comes

Many things ***will*** happen ***before*** Jesus comes back:

- Deceiving imposters will come to lead some astray (Matt. 24:4-5, 11, 24; Rev. 13:13-14).
- Wars and rumors of wars will happen (Dan. 9:26b; Matt. 24:6).
- Nation will fight against nation and kingdom against kingdom (Matt. 24:7).
- Famines and earthquakes will occur (Matt. 24:7).
- Believers will be persecuted (Matt. 24:9; Rev. 13:17; 14:9-10). (cf. Chapter 11)
- Love of most will grow cold (Matt. 24:12). (cf. Chapter 10)
- Gospel will be preached ***in*** the whole world (Matt. 24:14).
- The Temple will experience the abomination of desolation (Dan. 9:27; Matt. 24:15; Mark 13:14).
- Man of lawlessness [Antichrist] will be revealed (2 Thess. 2:1-12; Rev. 13:1-10).
- All the events of the Seal plagues will occur (Rev. 6:1-17; 8:1-5).
- All the events of the Trumpet plagues will happen (Rev. 8:6-21; 11:15-19).
- All the events of the Vial (Bowl) plagues will take place (Rev. 16:1-21).
- The sign of the Son of Man will appear in the sky (Matt. 24:30).
- A trumpet call will announce His coming (Matt. 24:31).

Many things ***must*** happen before Jesus comes back:

- all the events of the Tribulation cited above (e.g. Seal, Trumpet, and Vial plagues)
- gospel preached in the whole world
- snatching away of believers

When He Comes

He will:

- Stand on the Mount of Olives—from which He had ascended (Acts 1:11-12)—and it will split east to west (Zech. 14:4).
- Devastate Israel's enemies in the Battle of Armageddon (Rev. 16:16) and Valley of Jehoshaphat (Joel 3:1-2).
- Return with all of the previously raptured believers (Matt. 24:31).
- Judge the people living on earth at that time, separating them into *sheep* (righteous believers) and *goats* (wicked unbelievers) (Matt. 26:31-33). *Sheep* will be rewarded with heavenly fellowship and entrance into the kingdom prepared for them (Matt. 16:27; 26:34; 2 Thess. 2:1-4). *Goats* will be banished to the lake of fire (Matt. 26:41).
- Consign the Antichrist and the False Prophet to the lake of fire (burning sulfur) (Rev. 20:10).
- Incarceration of Satan in the Abyss for 1000 years (Rev. 20:1-2).

Cautionary Note

Tim LaHaye and Ed Hindson caution readers: "When reading the Bible's 320-plus references to the second coming, one must read the contents carefully to discern whether a specific passage is describing the rapture or the glorious appearing."[2]

Some, who write about the end times, confuse the second coming with the rapture and seem to meld them together. End-times authors Thomas Ice and Timothy Demy have devised a table to illustrate the differences.

Rapture / Translation	**Second Coming / Established Kingdom**
1. Translation of all believers	1. No translation at all
2. Translated saints go to heaven	2. Translated saints return to earth
3. Earth not judged	3. Earth judged and righteousness established
4. Imminent, any moment, signless	4. Follows definite predicted signs, including the Tribulation
5. Not in Old Testament	5. Predicted often in Old Testament
6. Believers only	6. Affects all humanity
7. Before the day of wrath	7. Concluding the day of wrath
8. No references to Satan	8. Satan bound
9. Christ comes for His own	9. Christ comes *with* His own
10. He comes in the *air*	10. He comes to the *earth*
11. He claims His bride	11. He comes with His bride
12. Only His own see Him	12. Every eye shall see Him
13. Tribulation begins	

Thomas Ice and Timothy Demy, used with author's permission

But God . . . !

CHAPTER 22

Armageddon

> [16] *Then they gathered the kings together to the place that in Hebrew is called Armageddon.*
>
> *(Rev. 16:16 NIV)*

The great end-time battle foretold to take place on the Plain of Jezreel in Israel is being discussed more and more. Some events have been suggested as embodying such a battle. Questions have been raised asking whether this event or another can be considered the epic battle.

Armageddon as a place name

The common English pronunciation of the Greek for *Armageddon* ignores the rough-breathing mark atop the "A." It is more properly pronounced with a hard "H" sound—*Harmageddon*. The Hebrew word "har" can mean *mountain* or *hill country*. Since there is no place called Mt. Megiddo, the meaning must fall closer to *hill-country* than *mountain*.[1] Megiddo is an actual place in Israel located on the slopes of the Valley of Jezreel—also called the Plain of Esdraelon.

The Valley of Jezreel is a place known in scripture for hosting battles. For example, Megiddo was a Canaanite fortress in the Plain of Jezreel captured by Israelites Deborah and Barak (Josh. 12:21; Judg. 5:19). Egyptian Pharoah Neco set out to conquer the Israelites, but was opposed in the valley of Megiddo by Israelite King Josiah (1 Chron. 35:20-22).

End-time teacher Robert L. Thomas notes:

> The plain of Megiddo is admittedly not large enough to contain armies from all over the world, so this must be the assembly area for a much larger deployment that covers a two hundred mile distance from north to south and the width of Palestine from east to west (cf. Zech. 14:20). Some decisive battles against this massive force will probably occur around Jerusalem (Zech. 14:1-3).[2]

Gathering place or battle place

Revelation 16:16 says Megiddo is a place where ***kings*** would ***gather*** for the final battle. Zechariah 14:2 says that Jerusalem is the place of which God says, "A day of the LORD is coming when your plunder will be divided among you. ***I will gather all the nations to Jerusalem*** to fight against it; the city will be captured, the houses ransacked, and the women raped." [Bold, italics mine]

Thomas is quoted above as saying, that the valley of Megiddo is not large enough to accommodate ***all the armies***. Can it be then, that Armageddon will be a ***gathering place*** to funnel troops into Jerusalem for the final attack?

To reinforce this view, Zechariah 12:1-4 (NIV) says:

> This is the word of the LORD concerning Israel. The LORD, who stretches out the heavens, who lays the foundation of the earth, and who forms the spirit of man within him, declares: "I am going to make Jerusalem a cup

> that sends all the surrounding peoples reeling. Judah will be besieged as well as Jerusalem. On that day, when all the nations of the earth are gathered against her, I will make Jerusalem an immovable rock for all the nations. All who try to move it will injure themselves. On that day I will strike every horse with panic and its rider with madness," declares the LORD. "I will keep a watchful eye over the house of Judah, but I will blind all the horses of the nations.

The phrase, *on that day*, points to the coming Day of the Lord.

Christ's Return

Christ's arrival on the Mount of Olives (cf. Zech. 14:4-5), just across the Kidron Valley from the Temple in Jerusalem suggests that Jerusalem, and not the Valley of Jezreel, will be the location of the final battle when Jesus finally decimates his enemy and exacts the consequences for unbelievers. Zech. 14:3 says, "Then the LORD will go out and fight against those nations, as he fights in the day of battle."

After His feet touch the Mount: (cf. Zech. 14:3-10)

- The mountain will split in two, east to west, forming a great valley.
- The Lord will return with all his holy ones (raptured believers).
- There will be no light, evening or nighttime, cold or frost.
- Living water will flow out of Jerusalem to the east (Dead Sea) and the west (Mediterranean Sea).
- The Lord will be king over all the earth.
- The land from Geba (just north ofJerusalem) to Rimmon (southwest of Jerusalem, and east of Masada—halfway to the Mediterranean) will become a vast plain.
- Jerusalem will be physically raised up.

When Jesus completes the final battle:

- Antichrist and the false prophet will be cast into the lake of fire (Rev. 19:20).
- Satan is bound and cast into the Abyss until the Millennium ends (Rev. 20:1-4).

The result of the final battle will be a massive bird banquet when an angel calls all the birds of the sky to come and clean up the dead flesh left after the battle (Rev. 19:17-18, 21).

But God . . . !

CHAPTER 23

Thousand Year Period

[1]And I saw an angel coming down out of heaven, having the key to the Abyss and holding in his hand a great chain. [2] He seized the dragon, that ancient serpent, who is the devil, or Satan, and bound him for a thousand years. [3] He threw him into the Abyss, and locked and sealed it over him, to keep him from deceiving the nations anymore until the thousand years were ended. After that, he must be set free for a short time. [4] I saw thrones on which were seated those who had been given authority to judge. And I saw the souls of those who had been beheaded because of their testimony for Jesus and because of the word of God. They had not worshiped the beast or his image and had not received his mark on their foreheads or their hands. They came to life and reigned with Christ a thousand years. [5] (The rest of the dead did not come to life until the thousand years were ended.) This is the first resurrection. (Rev. 20:1-5 NIV)

Following the end of the Tribulation (i.e. including the portion known as the Great Tribulation) will come a thousand year period called the Millennium. At the end of this period the world will experience a release of evil again for a brief time, followed by final judgment for mankind.

Millennial Positions

There is one tongue-in-cheek and three principle positions regarding the millennium:

- **Pan-Millennialism**—It will all *pan out* in the end—an unsophisticated, naïve, yet somewhat mirthful position.
- **Amillennialism**—there is no future millennium because the world is currently experiencing the *millennium* of Rev. 20. Amillennialists believe that the gospel is going forth and ultimately will infuse the entire world to accomplish the "gospel preached to the whole world" (Matt. 28:18).
- **Post-Millennialism**—Christ will return ***after*** the millennium.
- **Pre-Millennialism**—Christ will come back ***before*** the millennium.

This book takes a premillennial, pretribulation position which holds that:

- The *snatching away event* (*rapture*) will occur ***before*** the Tribulation (1 Thess. 4:16; 1 Cor. 15:51-53). (cf. Chapter 15)
- Christ will return to earth at the end of the Tribulation (Rev. 19:11-16).
- Satan will be bound for 1000 years (Rev. 20:1-3a).
- At the end of the 1000 year millennium:

- Satan will be loosed for a time to do his mischief (Rev. 20:3b, 7-9).
- Satan will be thrown into the lake of fire (Rev. 20:3b, 7-9).
- The remaining dead will be resurrected to be judged (Rev. 20:11-13).
- Those, whose names were not found in the book of life, were thrown into the lake of fire (Rev. 20:14-15).
- The New Jerusalem along with a new heaven and new earth will arrive (Rev. 21).

Satan Bound

Satan is removed from earth and prevented from engaging in more deception and persecution by being bound with chains and cast into the Abyss for one thousand years. Satan's work is terminated in the sphere of the earth during his confinement in the Abyss.

Earth's Population during the Millennium

The *New Westminster Dictionary of the Bible* states, "According to [Rev. 20], only the martyrs (vss. 4-5; cf. Ch. 13: 15) will rise and share with Christ this period of triumph and freedom from evil (Ch. 20: 3) before the final resurrection (v. 12). The privilege described in this chapter is considered as an honor that God bestows on those who have suffered for Christ."[1] This position is flawed in light of Zechariah 14:16 which speaks of, "everyone that is left of all the nations that have attacked Jerusalem" being present following the day of the Lord.

It appears then, that the inhabitants of the earth during the millennium will include:

- Jesus (Zech. 14:9)
- those given authority to judge (Rev. 20:4) (Commonly accepted to be the 24 elders, but more likely the members

of the army of Christ which returns with Him. These would then be the previously raptured believers.)

- resurrected souls beheaded for their faith (cf. Rev. 20:4)
- remaining people of the nations who were not killed during the Great Tribulation and battle of Armageddon—an unknown, but large number (Zech. 14:16)

Satan Loosed

After his release to deceive those deceivable ones, the devil will be thrown into the lake of burning sulfur—as were the Antichrist and False Prophet at the end of the Tribulation (Rev. 20:10).

Those deceived

The people who allowed themselves to be deceived by the devil tried to surround the camp of God's people and were subsequently killed by fire from heaven (Rev. 20:7-9).

Resurrection and judgment

The dead of the ages who were not believers will be resurrected and judged against the standard of a listing in the book of life (where the saved ones are listed) will be cast into the lake of burning sulfur (Rev. 20:11-15).

But God . . .

FINAL THOUGHTS

- What have we learned?
- Given the events currently happening and those prophesied for the future, how should we then live?

CHAPTER 24
Final Thoughts

> *[8] Do not let this Book of the Law depart from your mouth; meditate on it day and night, so that you may be careful to do everything written in it. Then you will be prosperous and successful.*
>
> (Josh. 1:8 NIV)
>
> *[22] Do not merely listen to the word, and so deceive yourselves. Do what it says. [23] Anyone who listens to the word but does not do what it says is like a man who looks at his face in a mirror [24] and, after looking at himself, goes away and immediately forgets what he looks like. [25] But the man who looks intently into the perfect law that gives freedom, and continues to do this, not forgetting what he has heard, but doing it--he will be blessed in what he does.*
>
> (James 1:22-25 NIV)

What have we learned?

We have learned:

- Bible prophecy and world events ***are*** converging. While only God knows the ***when*** of things, He has instructed us to remain alert for ***signs*** of the end times.
- Christians cannot bury their heads in the sand. Believers ***must*** avoid ignoring current events. God has given us a mission to spread the gospel message (Matt. 28:18-20). Yet we must avoid being so *heavenly-minded that we are no earthly good.*
- There is much going on *under the radar.* Just as with tsunamis, it may ***seem*** little is happening, but as the tsunami reaches shoal waters, things will get very bad, very fast.
- Jesus will return to take up His people. This is our blessed hope. He has promised it and He ***will*** fulfill it.
- Scripture ***is*** relevant to today's events.

So, what now?

Reading about the end-times is interesting and sometimes scary. Simply acquiring knowledge is insufficient.

Action is called for.

> And God said: "'Let there be light,' and there was light" (Gen. 1:3).—Believers are called to bring the light of the Gospel into the world. "You are the light of the world. A city on a hill cannot be hidden. Neither do people light a lamp and put it under a bowl. Instead they put it on its stand, and it gives light to everyone in the house. In the same way, let your light shine before men, that they may see your good deeds and praise your Father in heaven" (Matt. 5:14-16). Those of us who call ourselves Christians must

act like Christians and eschew behaving like the people of the world. Our morals and ethics must truly reflect Christ-likeness.

If, after having read *Spiritual Tsunami*, you became aware that you are not where God wants you to be spiritually, pray this prayer:

> Jesus, I know you love me unconditionally and that you gave your life for me as you died on the cross when I certainly did not deserve it. Please forgive me for my sins. I accept you as my Savior and from this day forth, freely choose to make you Lord in my life. All that I am is now yours for whatever purpose you have for me. Thank you for this. Amen.

The next step is to diligently study the scriptures to discover the signs Christ has given us to watch for in the last days.

There is a lot going on today; much of it *under the radar*, unreported in the media. Yet signs are available to discern what is going on. Some of them ***are*** being reported in diverse parts of the media. It requires a wide-ranging search of many forms of media coverage. Simply relying on American media coverage is insufficient as a result of bias. *BBC News* (United Kingdom & the world), *Al Jazeera* (Middle East), *Today's Kaman* (Turkey), *Tehran Times* (Iran), *Reuters*, etc. all provide analysis of current world news not covered by the American press.

For *Spiritual Tsunami*, the author had to research wide-ranging global media coverage to uncover events for which we have been forewarned in the Bible that are precursors and signs of these end-times. Much was not reported by American media because they are blinded to real events by the work of the enemy—Satan, " . . . Evil men and impostors will go from bad to worse, deceiving and being deceived" (2 Tim. 3:13 NIV).

And God . . .

- Has a plan which will succeed.
- Is always precise and true to His word.
- Has made provision for those who believe in and obey Him.

"For I know the plans I have for you," declares the LORD, "plans to prosper you and not to harm you, plans to give you hope and a future. Then you will call upon me and come and pray to me, and I will listen to you. You will seek me and find me when you seek me with all your heart" (Jer. 29:11-13 NIV).

One of the strongest commands Christ gave to last days believers is to **WATCH**! (cf. Matt. 24:42; 25:13; Mark 13:35-37; Luke 21:36)

Jesus warned end-times believers to, "Be careful—hearts may be worn down with":

- dissipation
- drunkenness
- anxieties of life

For, "that day will close on you unexpectedly like a trap" (Luke 21:34 NIV).

Watch!

Just as in the example of the ten virgins waiting for the arrival of the bridegroom; Christian believers must remain awake and alert with plenty of oil for their lamps. There will be no *recovery time* for those who are unprepared by vigilance and fellowship with the Holy Spirit (Matt. 25:8-10).

How Should We Live in the Last Days?

- "But just as he who called you is holy, so be holy in all you do" (1Pet. 1:15 NIV).

- "For you know that we dealt with each of you as a father deals with his own children, encouraging, comforting and urging you to live lives worthy of God, who calls you into his kingdom and glory" (1Thess. 2:11, 12 NIV).
- "But you are a chosen people, a royal priesthood, a holy nation, a people belonging to God, that you may declare the praises of him who called you out of darkness into his wonderful light" (1 Pet. 2:9 NIV).
- "For you were once darkness, but now you are light in the Lord. Live as children of light (for the fruit of the light consists in all goodness, righteousness and truth) and find out what pleases the Lord. Have nothing to do with the fruitless deeds of darkness, but rather expose them" (Eph. 5:8-11 NIV).
- "And this is my prayer: that your love may abound more and more in knowledge and depth of insight, so that you may be able to discern what is best and may be pure and blameless until the day of Christ, filled with the fruit of righteousness that comes through Jesus Christ—to the glory and praise of God" (Phil. 1:9-11 NIV).
- "In the same way, let your light shine before men, that they may see your good deeds and praise your Father in heaven" (Matt. 5:16 NIV).
- "So whether you eat or drink or whatever you do, do it all for the glory of God" (1 Cor. 10:31 NIV).

Our Blessed Hope

God's great salvation has made it possible for Christian believers to look forward with joyful anticipation to a blessed hope—the glorious appearing of our Lord Jesus Christ (Titus 2:13).

Maranatha! Come, Lord Jesus!

APPENDICES

- Graphic illustrations provide visual content that supports understanding.

APPENDIX A

Rapture Timelines

Pre-Tribulation Rapture Position

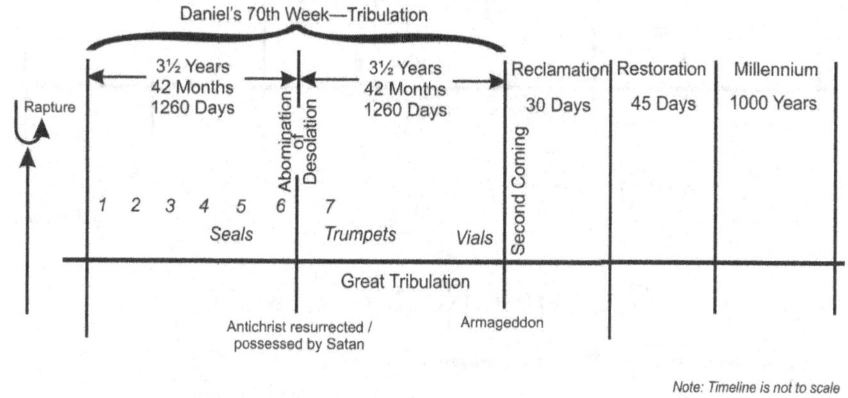

Post-Tribulation Rapture Position

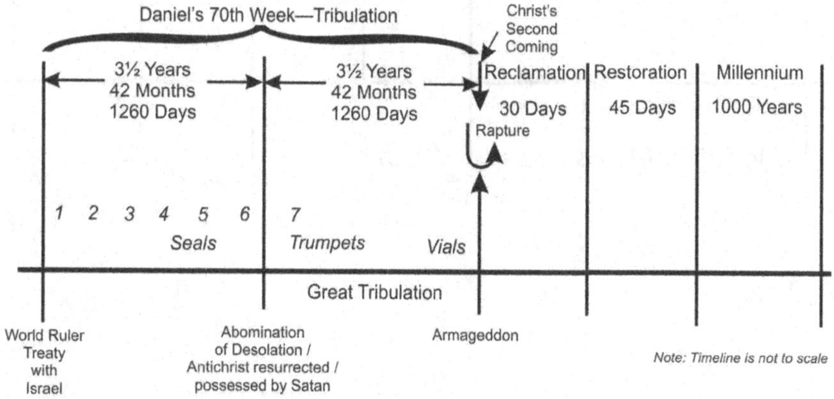

Mid-Tribulation Rapture Position

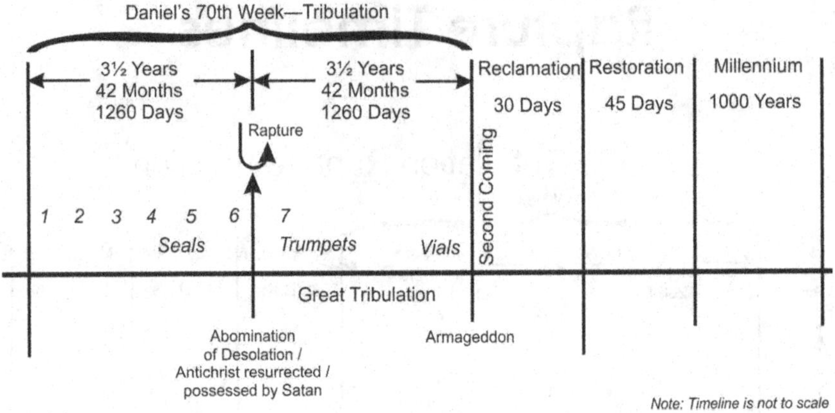

Pre-Wrath Rapture Position

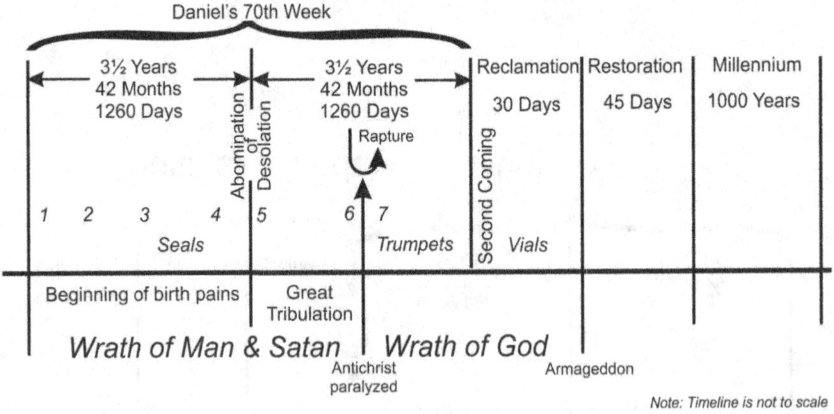

APPENDIX B

End Times Timeline With Rapture Views

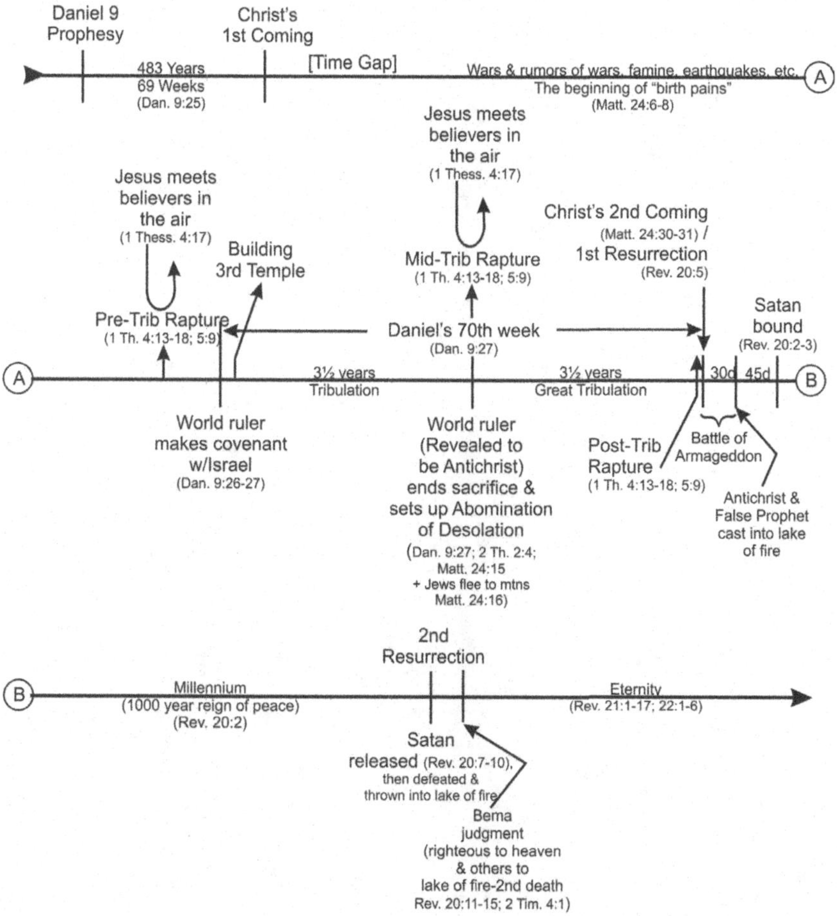

Daniel 9
Prophesy
Christ's
1st Coming
483 Years
69 Weeks
(Dan. 9:25)
[Time Gap]
Wars & rumors of wars, famine, earthquakes, etc.
The beginning of "birth pains"
(Matt. 24:6-8)
A
Jesus meets
believers in
the air
(1 Thess. 4:17)
Christ's 2nd Coming
(Matt. 24:30-31) /
1st Resurrection
(Rev. 20:5)
Jesus meets
believers in
the air
(1 Thess. 4:17)
Building
3rd Temple
Mid-Trib Rapture
(1 Th. 4:13-18; 5:9)
Pre-Trib Rapture
(1 Th. 4:13-18; 5:9)
Daniel's 70th week
(Dan. 9:27)
Satan
bound
(Rev. 20:2-3)
A
3½ years
Tribulation
3½ years
Great Tribulation
30d
45d
B
World ruler
makes covenant
w/Israel
(Dan. 9:26-27)
World ruler
(Revealed to
be Antichrist)
ends sacrifice &
sets up Abomination
of Desolation
(Dan. 9:27; 2 Th. 2:4;
Matt. 24:15
+ Jews flee to mtns
Matt. 24:16)
Post-Trib
Rapture
(1 Th. 4:13-18; 5:9)
Battle of
Armageddon
Antichrist &
False Prophet
cast into lake
of fire
2nd
Resurrection
B
Millennium
(1000 year reign of peace)
(Rev. 20:2)
Eternity
(Rev. 21:1-17; 22:1-6)
Satan
released (Rev. 20:7-10),
then defeated &
thrown into lake of fire
Bema
judgment
(righteous to heaven
& others to
lake of fire-2nd death
Rev. 20:11-15; 2 Tim. 4:1)

NOTES

Preface

[1] Dickens, Charles. "Quote from *Tale of Two Cities*." Accessed November 16, 2011. http://www.quotationspage.com/quote/29595.html.

Introduction

[1] McBride, Edward. Metropolis Magazine.com, "Monuments to Self." Last modified July 1999. Accessed July 14, 2011. http://www.metropolismag.com/html/content_0699/ju99monu.htm.

[2] Henry Snyder Gehman, *The New Westminster Dictionary of the Bible*, (Philadelphia, PA: The Westminster Press, 1983), 655-656.

[3] Wikipedia, the free encyclopedia, "Babylon." Accessed July 10, 2011. http://en.wikipedia.org/wiki/Babylon.

[4] MacLean, W.P. (2011) personal correspondence, "The influence of Multi-culturalism in our Educational system".

Chapter 1

[1] Oxfam International, "Global food prices in 2011: Questions & Answers." Accessed February 17, 2011. http://www.oxfam.org/en/campaigns/agriculture/food-price-crisis-questions-answers.

[2] Flavius Josephus, trans by William Whiston, The Works of Josephus: Complete and Unabridged, New Updated Edition, (Peabody, Massachusetts: Hendrickson Publishers, 1987), 546.

Chapter 2

[1] David Jeremiah, The Coming Economic Armageddon: What Bible Prophecy Warns about the New Global Economy, (New York: Faith Words/Hachette Book Group, 2010), 51.

[2] William Bonner, and Addison Wiggin, Empire of Debt, (Hoboken, New Jersey: John Wiley & Sons, Inc., 2006), 18.

[3] Oxfam International, "Global food prices in 2011: Questions & Answers." Accessed February 17, 2011. http://www.oxfam.org/en/campaigns/agriculture/food-price-crisis-questions-answers.

[4] Got Questions, "Does the Bible prophesy a one-world government and a one-world currency in the end times?." Accessed March 25, 2011. http://www.gotquestions.org/one-world-government.html.

[5] Time, "The World Food Crisis." Last modified November 1974. Accessed September 6, 2011. http://www.time.com/time/magazine/article/0,9171,911503-1,00.html.

[6] Reske, Henry, and Kathleen Walter. Newsmax TV, "Real Unemployment Near Depression Era Levels." Last modified October 7, 2011. Accessed October 10, 2011. http://www.newsmax.com/Headline/Trump-Kiyosaki-Unemployment-Depression/2011/10/07/id/413711?s=al&promo_code=D365-1.

[7] Trading Economics, "Statistics." Accessed November 2, 2011. http://www.tradingeconomics.com/unemployment-rates-list-by-country.

[8] David Weidmer, Robert A. Weidmer, and Cindy Spitzer, *Aftershock*, (Hobokan, New Jersey: John Wiley & Sons, Inc., 2011), 27-33.

[9] Ruddy, Christopher. Aftershock-NewsMax Memorandum, "Sir John Templeton's Last Testament: Financial Chaos Will Last Many Years." Last modified September 12,2011. Accessed September 14, 2011. https://mail.google.com/mail/?shva=1

[10] The Economist, "Silicon Valley and the technology industry—The new tech bubble." Last modified May 12, 2011. Accessed November 5, 2011. http://www.economist.com/node/18681576.

[11] Woo, Stu, Lynn Cowan, and Pui-Wing Tam. Wall Street Journal online, "LinkedIn IPO Soars, Feeding Web Boom." Last modified May 20, 2011. Accessed November 5, 2011. http://online.wsj.com/article/SB10001424052748704816604576333132239509622.html.

[12] Christie, Les. Yahoo Finance and CNN Money, "Home Prices Heading for Triple-Dip." Last modified October 31, 2011. Accessed October 31, 2011. http://finance.yahoo.com/real-estate/article/113725/home-prices-heading-triple-dip-cnnmoney?mod=realestate-sell.

[13] Pullella, Philip. Reuters, "Vatican urges economic reforms, condemns collective greed." Last modified October 31, 2011. Accessed November 2, 2011. : http://in.reuters.com/article/2011/10/24/idINIndia-60095120111024.

[14] The Economist, "Protests—Not quite together." Last modified October 22, 2011. Accessed November 5, 2011. http://www.economist.com/node/21533377.

[15] The Economist, "Capitalism and its critics—Rage against the machine." Last modified October 22, 2011. Accessed November 5, 2011. http://www.economist.com/node/21533400.

[16] Chapman, Steve. Chicago Tribune, "What Occupy Wall Street is getting totally wrong." Last modified November 6, 2011. Accessed November 6, 2011. http://www.chicagotribune.com/news/columnists/ct-oped-1106-chapman-20111106,0,5138167.column.

[17] Jones, Forrest. MoneyNews.com, "US Debt Eclipses Economic Output." Last modified November 21, 2011. Accessed November 23, 2011. http://www.moneynews.com/StreetTalk/US-Debt-Economic-Output/2011/11/21/id/418767?s=al&promo_code=D911-1.

[18] BBC News, "Eurozone debt web." Last modified November 18, 2011. Accessed November 20, 2011. http://www.bbc.co.uk/news/business-15748696.

[19] France24/Reuters, "Central banks join forces to ease euro debt crisis." Last modified November 30, 2011. Accessed November 30, 2011.

http://www.france24.com/en/20111130-central-banks-federal-reserve-finance-dollar-liquidity-eurozone-debt-crisis-imf-ecb.

[20] Los Angeles Times, "Central banks join forces to ease debt crisis." Last modified November 30, 2011. Accessed November 30, 2011. http://www.latimes.com/news/la-central-banks-m,0,3005331.story?track=rss.

Chapter 3

[1] Goldstein, Tani, and Avital Lahav. YNet News, "1.5 billion barrels of oil discovered near Rosh Ha'Ayin." Last modified August 17, 2010. Accessed August 18, 2011. http://www.ynetnews.com/articles/0,7340,L-3938192,00.html.

[2] Givot Olam Oil Co., "Bracha from the Lubavitcher Rebbe." Last modified November 27, 1988. Accessed August 11, 2010. http://www.givot.co.il/english/article.php?id=93.

[3] Mitchell, Chris. CBN.com, "A New Holy Oil? Searching for Petroleum in Israel." Last modified May 9, 2010. Accessed November 18, 2011. http://www.cbn.com/cbnnews/insideisrael/2010/May/Company-Searches-for-Oil-in-Israel/.

[4] Jerusalem Post, "Israel set to become gas exporter,." Last modified June 3, 2010. Accessed September 15, 2011. http://www.jpost.com/Business/BusinessNews/Article.aspx?id=177428.

Chapter 4

[1] See Introduction: Rebuilding of the Ancient City of Babylon

[2] Robson, Seth. Stars and Stripes, "U.S., Iraqi experts developing plan to preserve Babylon, build local tourism industry." Last modified June 28, 2009. Accessed June 30, 2009. http://www.stripes.com/news/u-s-iraqi-experts-developing-plan-to-preserve-babylon-build-local-tourism-industry-1.92976.

[3] Rosenberg, Joel. Joel Rosenberg's Flash Traffic, "Babylon Is Being Rebuilt, Just As Prophesied." Last modified June 29, 2009. Accessed June 30, 2009. http://flashtrafficblog.wordpress.com/page/5/.

Chapter 5

[1] Dictionary.com, "moral." Accessed August 09, 2011. http://dictionary.reference.com/browse/moral.

[2] Will Durant, The story of civilization. (Vol. I)., (New York: Simon and Schuster, 1963), 36.

[3] David Jeremiah, Living with Confidence in a Chaotic World, (Nashville, Tenn.: Thomas Nelson, 2009), 117.

[4] op cit, 120-121.

[5] George Barna, Futurecast, (Carol Stream, Illinois: BarnaBooks/Tyndale House Publishers, Inc., 2011), chap. 3.

[6] ibid.

[7] Charles, Tyler. Relevant Magazine, "(Almost) everyone's doing it." Last modified Sept-Oct 2011 issue. Accessed October 6, 2011. http://issuu.com/relevantmagazine/docs/sept_oct_2011/66?mode=a_p

[8] Pew Research Center, "The Decline of Marriage And Rise of New Families." Last modified November 8, 2010. Accessed October 25, 2011. http://pewsocialtrends.org.

[9] ibid.

[10] U.S. Census Bureau, "Unmarried Partners of the Opposite Sex." Last modified November 2010. Accessed January 2, 2012. http://www.census.gov/population/www/socdemo/hh-fam.html

[11] Popenoe, David, and Barbara Dafoe Whitehead. Rutgers University, "National Marriage Project." Last modified 2008. Accessed October 24, 2011. http://www.virginia.edu/marriageproject/specialreports.html.

[12] Pew Research Center, "The Decline of Marriage And Rise of New Families." Last modified November 8, 2010. Accessed October 25, 2011. http://pewsocialtrends.org.

[13] Trendwatch.com, "Trend driver—Casual Collapse." Last modified 2011. Accessed August 28, 2011. http://trendwatching.com/briefing/.

[14] BBC News, "Cameron threat to dock some UK aid to anti-gay nations." Last modified October 30, 2011. Accessed October 30, 2011. http://www.bbc.co.uk/news/uk-15511081.

[15] Whitley, Joseph Garland. The College of William and Mar, "Reversing the Perceived Moral Decline in American Schools: A Critical Literature Review of America's Attempt at Character Education." Accessed August 5, 2011. http://www.characterfirst.com/.

[16] Quinn, Ben. The Guardian UK, ".& Adult Entertainment Domain Approved by Internet Regulators." Last modified March 19, 2911. Accessed March 23, 2011. http://www.guardian.co.uk/technology/2011/mar/19/&-domain-suffix-adult-entertainment/print.

[17] BBC News, "Porn sites sue internet regulator over & web address." Last modified November 21, 2011. Accessed November 21, 2011. http://www.bbc.co.uk/news/technology-15816630.

[18] Office of the United Nations High Commissioner for Human Rights, "Convention on the Rights of the Child." Accessed November 28, 2011. http://www2.ohchr.org/english/law/crc.htm.

[19] ibid.

[20] ParentalRights.org, "UN Convention on the Rights of the Child." Accessed November 28, 2011. http://www.parentalrights.org/index.asp?Type=B_BASIC&SEC={EFFB5B62-5D8F-4F60-959A-F5D42FCB863F}&DE=.

[21] ParentalRights.org, "The Supreme Court's Parental Rights Doctrine." Accessed November 28, 2011. http://www.parentalrights.org/index.asp?Type=B_BASIC&SEC={12D52BF9-1D6D-4EEC-B83B-F74B3F91BDF6}&DE=.

[22] John Piper, Desiring God, (Sisters, Oregon: Multnomah Books, 1996), 173.

Chapter 6

[1] Dictionary.com, "ethics." Accessed August 09, 2011. http://dictionary.reference.com/browse/moral.

[2] Frank, Robert, and Amir Efrati. Wall Street Journal online, "'Evil' Madoff Gets 150 Years in Epic Fraud." Last modified June 30, 2009. Accessed October 28, 2011. http://online.wsj.com/article/SB124604151653862301.html.

[3] Milburn, John. Kansas City Star, "Kansas secretary of state fined $5,000 for errors in campaign reports." Last modified October 26,2011. Accessed October 28, 2011. http://www.kansascity.com/2011/10/26/3231504/kobachs-2010-campaign-fined-5000.html.

[4] Trendwatch.com, "Trend driver—Casual Collapse." Last modified 2011. Accessed August 28, 2011. http://trendwatching.com/briefing/.

[5] Transparency International, "CORRUPTION PERCEPTIONS INDEX 2010." Accessed December 10, 2010. http://www.transparency.org/policy_research/surveys_indices/cpi/2010/results.

[6] Organization for Economic Co-operation and Development (OECD)., "Fighting Corruption in the Public Sector." Accessed December 10, 2010. http://www.oecd.org/document/2/0,3746, en_2649_34135_41880322_1_1_1_1,00.html.

[7] Vogelwede & Associates, "Corruption Control Consultants." Accessed October 28, 2011. http://www.corruptioncontrol.com/.

[8] Knowledge@Wharton (Business Ethics), "How Bribery and Other Types of Corruption Threaten the Global Marketplace." Accessed October 28, 2011. http://knowledge.wharton.upenn.edu/article.cfm?articleid=646.

[9] The Economist, "Corruption—Grand Schemes." Last modified October 26, 2011. Accessed October 26, 2011. http://www.economist.com/node/21534761.

[10] The Economist, "Psychology—All power tends to corrupt." Last modified October 1, 2011. Accessed November 4, 2011. http://www.economist.com/node/21530945.

[11] NewsMax.com, "Egyptian Military Using Nerve Gas on Protesters." Last modified November 23, 2011. Accessed November 23, 2011.

http://www.newsmax.com/Newsfront/egyptian-military-nerve-gas/2011/11/23/id/418927?s=al&promo_code=D935-1.

[12] Kincaid, Cliff. GOPUSA.com, "Why Do Media Hate the Police?." Last modified November 23, 2011. Accessed November 23, 2011. http://www.gopusa.com/commentary/2011/11/23/kincaid-why-do-media-hate-the-police/?subscriber=1.

[13] United States Senate, "Oath of Office." Accessed November 28, 2011. http://www.senate.gov/artandhistory/history/common/briefing/Oath_Office.htm.

[14] House of Representatives, "Oath of Office." Accessed November 28, 2011. http://clerk.house.gov/member_info/oathoffice.aspx.

[15] Farris, Michael P. ParentalRights.org, "The UN Convention on the Rights of the Child: The Impact on Private Gun-Ownership in America." Last modified May 11, 2009. Accessed November 29, 2011. http://www.parentalrights.org/index.asp?Type=B_BASIC&SEC={96190840-EC3B-4A5E-80EE-9719625B62A5}.

[16] Fox News, "Solyndra Case Reveals Gateway Between Administration Loans, Obama Allies." Last modified November 16, 2011. Accessed December 21, 2011. http://www.foxnews.com/politics/2011/11/16/solyndra-case-reveals-gateway-between-administration-loans-obama-allies/.

[17] Mosk, Matthew, Brian Ross, and Ronnie Greene. ABC Good Morning America, "Emails: Obama White House Monitored Huge Loan to 'Connected' Firm." Last modified September 13, 2011. Accessed December 21, 2011. http://abcnews.go.com/Blotter/emails-obama-white-house-monitored-huge-loan-connected/story?id=14508865

[18] Boyle, Matthew. Fox News/The Daily Caller, "Daily Caller Draws Michelle Obama Connection to Solyndra." Last modified September 19, 2011. Accessed December 21, 2011. http://nation.foxnews.com/solyndra/2011/09/19/daily-caller-draws-michele-obama-connection-solyndra.

[19] Stephens, Joe, and Carol D. Leonnig. The Washington Post, "Solyndra e-mails show Obama fundraiser discussed lobbying White House." Last modified November 9, 2011. Accessed December 21, 2011. http://www.washingtonpost.com/politics/solyndra-e-mails-show-obama-fundraiser-discussed-lobbying-white-house/2011/11/09/gIQAqPsq5M_story.html.

[20] Macey, Jonathon. Wall Street Journal online, "Congress's Phony Insider-Trading Reform." Last modified December 13, 2011. Accessed January 8, 2012. http://online.wsj.com/article/SB10001424052970203413304577088881987346976.html.

[21] Margasak, Larry. Huffington Post, "Congress Looking At Insider Trading Laws." Last modified November 30, 2011. Accessed January 8, 2012. http://www.huffingtonpost.com/2011/11/30/insider-trading-congress-stock-act_n_1121675.html.

[22] Chicago Tribune, "Speaking of free marketeers . . . ." Last modified January 4, 2011. Accessed January 8, 2012. http://www.chicagotribune.com/news/opinion/editorials/ct-edit-markets2-76-lines-jm-20120104,0,3387020.story.

[23] Lee, M.J. Politico.com, "Rick Perry: End Congress insider trading." Last modified January 6, 2012. Accessed January 8, 2012. http://www.politico.com/news/stories/0112/71142.html.

[24] O'Toole, James. CNN Money, "Congress takes on insider trading. by Congress." Last modified December 7, 2011. Accessed January 8, 2012. http://money.cnn.com/2011/12/07/news/congress_insider_trading/index.htm.

[25] ibid.

[26] ibid.

Chapter 7

[1] John Hagee, Can America Survive?, (New York: Howard Books, 2010), 127-128.

[2] Lee, MJ. Politico.com, "McCain blasts 'hot mic' on Netanyahu." Last modified November 8, 2011. Accessed November 20, 2011. http://www.politico.com/news/stories/1111/67839.html.

[3] David Jeremiah, I Never Thought I'd See the Day, (New York: Faith Words/Hachette Book Group, 2011), 246.

[4] Arsu, Sebne, Isabel Kershner, and Alan Cowell. New York Times, "Turkey Expels Israeli Envoy in Dispute Over Raid." Last modified September 11, 2011. Accessed September 11, 2011. http://www.nytimes.com/2011/ 09/03/world/middleeast/03turkey.html.

[5] Bronner, Ethan. New York Times, "Beyond Cairo, Israel Sensing a Wider Siege." Last modified September 10, 2011. Accessed September 11, 2011. http://www.nytimes.com/2011/09/11/world/middleeast/11israel.html?pagewanted=1&_r=1.

[6] Anti-Defamation League, "Iran's President Mahmoud Ahmadinejad in his Own Words." Last modified August 26, 2011. Accessed November 26, 2011. http://www.adl.org/main_International_Affairs/ahmadinejad_words.htm?Multi_page_sections=sHeading_1.

[7] Hafezi, Parisa. Reuters.com, "Q&A: How powerful is the Iranian president?." Last modified June 11, 2009. Accessed November 26, 2011. http://www.reuters.com/article/2009/05/26/us-iran-election-president-qanda-sb-idUSTRE54P1QV20090526.

Chapter 8

[1] Joel Rosenberg, Epicenter 2.0 Version, (Carol Stream, Illinois: Tyndale House Publishers, Inc., 2008), xv-xvi.

[2] Dareini, Ali Akbar. Boston Globe/Boston.com, "Iran threatens to hit Turkey if US, Israel attack." Last modified November 26, 2011. Accessed November 26, 2011. http://www.boston.com/news/world/middleeast/articles/2011/11/26/iran_threatens_to_hit_turkey_if_us_israel_attack/.

[3] Miller, Sarah, and Haaretz Service. Haaretz, "Netanyahu: Nuclear-armed Iran is the greatest danger facing Israel." Last modified August 8, 2010. Accessed December 24, 2011. http://www.haaretz.com/news/

diplomacy-defense/netanyahu-nuclear-armed-iran-is-the-greatest-danger-facing-israel-1.323642.

[4] MoneyNews.com, "Iran Threatens to Stop Gulf Oil if Sanctions Widened." Last modified December 27,2011. Accessed December 27, 2011. http://www.moneynews.com/StreetTalk/Iran-Oil-Flow-Sanctions/2011/12/27/id/422219?s=al&promo_code=DCB7-1.

[5] Eldar, Akiva. Haaretz, "Palestinian PM to Haaretz: We will have a state next year." Last modified December 29, 2010. Accessed December 30, 2010. http://www.haaretz.com/print-edition/news/palestinian-pm-to-haaretz-we-will-have-a-state-next-year-1.283802.

[6] Cooper, Helene. New York Times, "Obama Says Palestinians Are Using Wrong Forum." Last modified September 21, 2011. Accessed December 23, 2011. http://www.nytimes.com/2011/09/22/world/obama-united-nations-speech.html.

[7] ibid.

[8] McGreal, Chris. UK Guardian, "UN vote on Palestinian state put off amid lack of support." Last modified November 11, 2011. Accessed December 23, 2011. http://www.guardian.co.uk/world/2011/nov/11/united-nations-delays-palestinian-statehood-vote.

Chapter 9

[1] MacLean, W.P. (2011) personal correspondence, "The influence of Multi-culturalism in our Educational system".

[2] Rocca, Francis X. Washington Post, "Vatican blasts 'idolatry' of global markets." Last modified October 24, 2011. Accessed October 26, 2011. http://www.washingtonpost.com/national/on-faith/vatican-blasts-idolatry-of-global-markets/2011/10/24/gIQAxh4UDM_story.html.

[3] United Nations, "World Economic and Social Survey." Last modified 2010. Accessed November 26, 2011. http://www.un.org/esa/policy/wess/wess2010files/wess2010.pdf.

[4] Joshua Goldstein, Winning the War on War: The Decline of Armed Conflict Worldwide, (New York: Dutton, 2011), 308, 316.

[5] ibid, 321

[6] ibid, 322

[7] ibid, 323, 324

[8] ibid, 325

[9] ibid, 326, 327

[10] Hal Lindsay, with C.C. Carlson, The Late Great Planet Earth, (Grand Rapids, Michigan: Zondervan Publishing House, 1970), 94.

[11] Mark Hitchcock, The Amazing Claims of Bible Prophecy, (Eugene, Oregon: Harvest House Publishers, 2010), 112.

[12] ibid, 113

[13] Wojtasiak, Steve. Seagate Technology, "Why smarter people precedes smarter storage." Last modified August 24, 2011. Accessed January 11, 2012. http://storageeffect.media.seagate.com/2011/08/storage-effect/why-smarter-people-precedes-smarter-storage/.

[14] Wojtowecz, Steve. Forbes, "To Manage Big Data, You Need Smarter Storage." Last modified August 22, 2011. Accessed January 11, 2012. http://blogs.forbes.com/ciocentral/?p=2516.

[15] Wojtasiak, Steve. Seagate Technology, "It's not just a hard drive, it's a treasure map." Last modified August 25, 2011. Accessed January 11, 2012. http://storageeffect.media.seagate.com/2011/03/storage-effect/its-not-just-a-hard-drive-its-a-treasure-map/.

[16] Mark Hitchcock, Who Is the Antichrist: Answering the Question Everyone is Asking, (Eugene, Oregon: Harvest House Publishers, 2011), 77.

[17] Good exegesis requires understanding words in context and firmly establishing them with multiple sources. (Deut. 17:6; Matt. 18:16) When reading the newspaper, it is essential to avoid simply accepting a word used in an article as meaning the same thing in one's own culture that it does in scripture.

[18] op cit. 113.

[19] ibid. 115

[20] ibid. 117

[21] ibid. 118

[22] ibid. 121

[23] ibid. 125

[24] ibid. 179

[25] David Jeremiah, What in the World is Going On?, (Nashville, Tenn.: Thomas, 2008), 123.

[26] Ice, Thomas. pre-trib.org, "Is America In Bible Prophecy?." Last modified n.d. Accessed January 14, 2012. http://www.pre-trib.org/articles/view/is-america-in-Bible-prophecy.

[27] Mark Hitchcock, The Late Great United States, (Colorado Springs, Colorado: Multnomah Books, 2009), 30-31.

[28] Terry James, The American Apocalypse, (Eugene, Oregon: Harvest House Publishers, 2009), 20-21.

[29] Stein, Ben. The American Spectator, "One World Government Obama." Last modified March 22, 2011. Accessed March 25, 2011. http://spectator.org/archives/2011/03/22/one-world-government-obama.

[30] Unknown. oneworldgovernment.org, "One World Government." Last modified September 4, 2010. Accessed March 25, 2011. http://oneworldgovernment.org/.

[31] ibid.

[32] Bauer, Mike. frontpagemag.com, "Obama's Czars and Their Left-Wing Affiliations." Last modified May 16, 2011. Accessed January 15, 2012. http://frontpagemag.com/2011/05/16/obama's-czars-and-their-left-wing-affiliations/1/.

[33] ibid.

[34] ibid.

Chapter 10

[1] apostasy. Dictionary.com. *Collins English Dictionary—Complete & Unabridged 10th Edition.* HarperCollins Publishers. http://dictionary.reference.com/browse/apostasy(accessed: December 25, 2011).

[2] Dyck, Drew. Christianity Today, "The Leavers." Last modified November 2010. Accessed November 8, 2011. http://www.christianitytoday.com/ct/2010/november/27.40.html?start=1.

[3] Pew Research Center, Pew Forum on Religion and Public Life, "Religion among the Millennials." Last modified February 2010. Accessed August 15, 2011. http://pewforum.org/Age/Religion-Among-the-Millennials.aspx.

[4] Barna Group, "Barna Study of Religious Change Since 1991 Shows Significant Changes by Faith Group." Last modified August 4, 2011. Accessed November 24, 2011. http://www.barna.org/faith-spirituality/514-barna-study-of-religious-change-since-1991-shows-significant-changes-by-faith-group.

[5] Dyck, Drew. buildingchurchleaders.com, "The Ones Who Walk Away." Last modified October 19, 2010. Accessed November 8, 2010. http://www.buildingchurchleaders.com/downloads/practicalministryskills/reachmillennialsfaith/ps89-a.html.

Chapter 11

[1] 10 News.com, "Couple: County Trying To Stop Home Bible Studies." Last modified May 28, 2009. Accessed December 3, 2011. www.10news.com/news/19562217/detail.html.

[2] David Jeremiah, Living with Confidence in a Chaotic World, (Nashville, Tenn.: Thomas Nelson, 2009), 161-162.

[3] Open Doors International, "2011 World Watchlist." Accessed December 3, 2011. http://www.opendoorsuk.org/resources/documents/WorldWatchList.pdf.

[4] The Economist, "Religious freedom: Christians and lions." Last modified December 30, 2011. Accessed January 14, 2012. http://www.economist.com/node/21542195?fsrc=scn/tw/te/.

Chapter 12

[1] Missler, Chuck. "Seven Mysterious Letters." Koinonia House eNews, November 5, 2008. https://mail.google.com/mail/?shva=1

[2] John F. Walvoord, Revised and Edited by Philip E. Rawley, and Mark Hitchcock, Revelation: Revised and Edited, (Chicago: Moody Publishers, 2011), 52.

[3] Robert L. Thomas, Revelation 1-7: An Exegetical Commentary, Kenneth Barker, General Editor, (Chicago: Moody Press, 1992), 125-126.

[4] ibid. 127.

[5] ibid. 127.

[6] op. cit. 52

Chapter 13

[1] Achenbach, Joel. The Washington Post, "Japan's 'black swan'." Last modified March 1, 2011. Accessed March 27, 2011. http://www.washingtonpost.com/national/japans-black-swan-scientists-ponder-the-unparalleled-dangers-of-unlikely-disasters/2011/03/17/ABj2wTn_story_1.html.

[2] ibid.

[3] Borenstein, Seth, and Julie Reed Bell. The Salt Lake Tribune, "2010's world gone wild: Quakes, floods, blizzards." Last modified December 19, 2010. Accessed December 12, 2010. http://www.sltrib.com/csp/cms/sites/sltrib/pages/printerfriendly.csp?id=50904909.

[4] ibid.

[5] Scott, Michon. NASA, "NASA Map Tracks Heavy Rainfall from Typhoon Megi." Last modified October 27, 2010. Accessed December 30,

2010. http://www.nasa.gov/mission_pages/hurricanes/archives/2010/h2010_Megi.html.

[6] Borenstein, Seth, and Julie Reed Bell. Op cit.

[7] Barcott, Bruce. Outside Magazine, "Totally Psyched For the Full-Rip Nine." Last modified August 25, 2011. Accessed September 12, 2011. http://www.outsideonline.com/outdoor-adventure/nature/Totally-Psyched-for-the-Full-Rip-Nine.html?page=1.

[8] Nir, Sarah Maslin. New York Times, "For a Weekend, Oklahoma is Earthquake Country." Last modified November 6, 2011. Accessed November 6, 2011. http://www.nytimes.com/2011/11/07/us/oklahoma-earthquake-sets-a-record.html?_r=1&ref=earthquakes.

[9] Burch, Jonathon. Yahoo News, "Strong earthquake hits Turkey, up to 1,000 feared killed." Last modified October 23, 2011. Accessed October 26, 2011. http://news.yahoo.com/magnitude-7-6-earthquake-hits-eastern-turkey-usgs-105909849.html.

[10] Fox News, "Strong Earthquake Hits Southern Iran, 6 Killed." Last modified December 21, 2010-. Accessed December 30, 2010. http://www.foxnews.com/world/2010/12/20/strong-earthquake-hits-southeastern-iran/.

[11] Sinoski, Kelly, and Gordon Hoekstra. The Vancouver Sun, "Earthquake off Vancouver Island felt in Metro Vancouver." Last modified September 9, 2011. Accessed December 4, 2011. http://www.vancouversun.com/news/Earthquake Vancouver Island felt Metro Vancouver/5378684/story.html.

[12] USGS, "USGS Earthquake Information-Significant earthquakes." Accessed March 27, 2011. http://earthquake.usgs.gov/.

[13] Dolak, Kevin. ABC News, "Northern Lights Seen Across Southeast U.S." Last modified October 25, 2011. Accessed October 25, 2011. http://gma.yahoo.com/blogs/abc-blogs/northern-lights-seen-across-southeast-u-054052417.html.

[14] BBC News—Science and Environment, "Solar flare was sparked by five spinning sunspots." Last modified April 20, 2011. Accessed April 21, 2011. http://www.bbc.co.uk/news/science-environment-13131535.

[15] Redd, Nola Taylor. Yahoo News/Space.com, "2011 Was the Year of the Restless Sun." Last modified December 29, 2011. Accessed December 30, 2011. http://news.yahoo.com/2011-restless-sun-130503012.html.

[16] ibid.

[17] Burns, Judith. BBC News—Science and Environment, "Sun storms 'could be more disruptive within decades'." Last modified August 18, 2011. Accessed August 22, 2011. http://www.bbc.co.uk/news/science-environment-14580995.

[18] US Geological Survey, "Overview of the ARkStorm Scenario: Multihazards Demonstration Project." Last modified January 24, 2011. Accessed March 27, 2011. http://pubs.usgs.gov/of/2010/1312/.

[19] Bluestein, Greg, and Jay Reeves. Associated Press/Yahoo! News, "Dozens of tornadoes kill 209 in 6 Southern states." Last modified April 28, 2011. Accessed April 28, 2011. http://news.yahoo.com/s/ap/us_severe_weather.

[20] infoplease.com, "Common Infectious Diseases Worldwide." Last modified 2007. Accessed September 8, 2009. http://www.infoplease.com/ipa/A0903696.html.

[21] World Health Organization, "Smallpox: Historical Significance." Last modified 2001. Accessed December 8, 2009.

[22] Centers for Disease Control, "World Health Day 2011: Antimicrobial Resistance." Last modified 2011. Accessed December 5, 2011. http://www.cdc.gov/features/WorldHealthDay/.

[23] personalliberty.com, "Expert warns of new drug-resistant bacteria in hospitals." Last modified November 19, 2008. Accessed December 9, 2008. http://www.personalliberty.com/news/expert-warns-of-new-drug-resistant-bacteria-in-hospitals-18885506/.

Chapter 14

[1] Drummond, Katie. Wired Magazine, "Pentagon Looks to Breed Immortal 'Synthetic Organisms,' Molecular Kill-Switch Included." Last modified February 2, 2010. Accessed August 25, 2011. http://www.wired.com/dangerroom/2010/02/pentagon-looks-to-breed-immortal-synthetic-organisms-molecular-kill-switch-included/.

[2] ibid.

[3] Hirschler, Ben. Reuters.com, "New rules urged on hybrid animal-human experiments." Last modified July 21, 2011. Accessed October 12, 2011. http://www.reuters.com/article/2011/07/21/us-science-animal-human-idUSTRE76K7Q220110721.

[4] Berkowitz, Bonnie. The Washington Post, "3-D printers may someday allow labs to create replacement human organs." Last modified May 9, 2011. Accessed May 12, 2011. http://www.washingtonpost.com/national/science/3-d-printers-may-someday-allow-labs-to-create-replacment-human-organs/2011/04/21/AFJM0WbG_print.html.

[5] Sorensen, Eric. Washington State University, "3D printer used to make bone-like material." Last modified November 29, 2011. Accessed December 7, 2011. http://news.wsu.edu/pages/publications.asp?Action=Detail&PublicationID=29002.

[6] Tomek, Allison. VeriChip Corporation, "VeriChip Corporation Selected by Microsoft to Offer Personal Health Record through Microsoft HealthVault." Last modified November 19, 2008. Accessed November 27, 2008. http://www.verichipcorp.com/news/1227122000.

[7] BusinessWire.com, "PositiveID Corporation Changes Ticker Symbol to PSID and Unveils New Logo." Last modified November 11, 2009. Accessed November 19, 2009. http://www.businesswire.com/portal/site/google/?ndmViewId=news_view&newsId=20091111005320&newsLang=en.

[8] Maney, Kevin. USA Today, "Get chipped, then charge without plastic—you are the card." Last modified May 12, 2004. Accessed November 9,

2009. http://www.usatoday.com/money/industries/technology/maney/2004-05-12-chip_x.htm?POE=click-refer.

[9] Ahlberg, Liz. University of Illinois at Urbana-Champaign, "Smart skin: Electronics that stick and stretch like a temporary tattoo." Last modified August 11, 2011. Accessed August 15, 2011. http://www.eurekalert.org/pub_releases/2011-08/uoia-sse080511.php.

[10] Edwards, Jim. CBS News, "Microchip Implant Controversy: a Mark of the Beast or the Coming "Singularity"?." Last modified October 9, 2009. Accessed November 20, 2009. http://www.cbsnews.com/8301-505123_162-42843185/microchip-implant-controversy-a-mark-of-the-beast-or-the-coming-singularity/?tag=bnetdomain.

[11] ibid.

[12] Rohde & Schwarz, "1MA182: Near Field Communication (NFC) Technology and Measurements." Last modified March 2011. Accessed December 10, 2011. http://www2.rohde-schwarz.com/en/service_and_support/Downloads/Application_Notes/?downid=7019.

[13] "Advertisement: Near Field Communication—No Life Untouched." Forbes, December 19, 2011, n.p.

Chapter 15

[1] Pew Research Center, Pew Forum on Religion and Public Life, "Global Survey of Evangelical Protestant Leaders." Last modified June 2011. Accessed December 9, 2011. http://pewforum.org/Christian/Evangelical-Protestant-Churches/Global-Survey-of-Evangelical-Protestant-Leaders.aspx.

[2] ibid.

[3] ibid.

[4] John F. Walvoord, *Every Prophecy of the Bible*, (Colorado Springs, Colorado: David C. Cook, 1999), Author Credits.

[5] Marvin Rosenthal, The Pre-Wrath Rapture of the Church, (Nashville, Tenn.: Thomas Nelson Publishers, 1990), 53.

6 ibid. pp.53-54

[7] Ice, Thomas. according2prophecy.org, "The Rapture and The Second Coming: An Important Distinction." Last modified n.d. Accessed December 9, 2011. http://www.according2prophecy.org/rapsec.html.

[8] Ice, Thomas. according2prophecy.org, "Perhaps Today: The Imminent Coming of Christ." Last modified n.d. Accessed December 13, 2011. http://www.according2prophecy.org/perhaps.html.

[9] Warner, Tim. Oasis Christian Church, "Eschatology of the Post-Apostolic Church." Last modified May 2, 2008. Accessed December 12, 2011. http://www.oasischristianchurch.org/air/018.pdf.

[10] Wikipedia, the free encyclopedia, "Robert Van Kampen." Last modified November 22, 2011. Accessed December 14, 2011. http://en.wikipedia.org/wiki/Robert_Van_Kampen.

[11] imminence. Dictionary.com. *Collins English Dictionary—Complete & Unabridged 10th Edition*. HarperCollins Publishers. http://dictionary.reference.com/browse/imminence (accessed: December 21, 2011).

[12] impending. Dictionary.com. *Collins English Dictionary—Complete & Unabridged 10th Edition*. HarperCollins Publishers. http://dictionary.reference.com/browse/impending (accessed: December 21, 2011).

[13] J. Daniel Hays, J. Scott Duvall, and C. Marvin Pate, Dictionary of Biblical Prophecy and End Times, (Grand Rapids, Michigan: Zondervan Publishing House, 2007), 208-209.

Chapter 16

[1] Ehrlich, Ines. YNet News, "Modern day Gog and Magog." Last modified December 10, 2006. Accessed July 26, 2010. http://www.ynetnews.com/articles/0,7340, L-3338175,00.html.

[2] Ronen, Gil. Arutz Sheva 7, "Rabbis: Flotilla Clash Similar to Gog and Magog Prophecy." Last modified June 10, 2010. Accessed June 10, 2010.

[3] Rosenberg, Joel C. Joel Rosenberg's Flash Traffic, "Putin Rising: But is he "Gog"?." Last modified August 17, 2011. Accessed August 18, 2011. http://flashtrafficblog.wordpress.com/2011/08/17/putin-rising-but-is-he-gog/.

[4] The Economist, "Political crisis in Russia: Voting, Russian-style." Last modified December 10, m2011. Accessed December 16, 2011. http://www.economist.com/node/21541455.

Chapter 17

[1] Israel Birding, "Griffin Vulture Information." Last modified n.d. Accessed July 28, 2011. http://www.birds.org.il/872-en/Birding-Israel.aspx.

[2] Fisher, Gary. Lion of Judah Ministries, "Flesh-Eating Birds Gather In Israel." Last modified February 20, 2010. Accessed December 16, 2011. http://www.watchmanscry.com/forum/showthread.php?t=8335.

[3] Rinat, Zafrir. Haaretz, "Israel asks world for help as vulture population dwindles." Last modified September 16, 2011. Accessed December 17, 2011. http://www.haaretz.com/print-edition/news/israel-asks-world-for-help-as-vulture-population-dwindles-1.384728.

[4] Walker, Bob. BBC News, "Biblical vulture's Holy Land struggle." Last modified August 25, 2010. Accessed December 17, 2011. http://news.bbc.co.uk/today/hi/today/newsid_8943000/8943167.stm.

Chapter 18

[1] Rosenberg, J. (2008). *Epicenter*: why the current rumblings in the Middle East will change your future. Carol Stream, IL: Tyndale House Pub.

[2] *Guide to ascending the Mount,* (n.d.). Retrieved Aug 2011 from http://www.templeinstitute.org/guide_to_ascending_the_mount.htm

[3] Rev.S.D.F. Salmond, "Part II.—Dogmatical and Historical. Treatise on Christ and Antichrist," The Anti-Nicene Fathers, Vol. V. ed. The Rev. Alexander Roberts, D.D., and James Donaldson, LL.D. (Grand Rapids, Michigan: Wm. B. Eerdmans Publishing Company, 1978), 206.

Chapter 19

[1] Wikipedia, the free encyclopedia, "List of people claimed to be Jesus." Last modified December 22, 2011. Accessed December 22, 2011. http://en.wikipedia.org/wiki/List_of_people_who_have_claimed_to_be_Jesus.

Chapter 20

[1] John F. Walvoord, Revelation: Revised and Edited by Philip E. Rawley, and Mark Hitchcock, (Chicago: Moody Publishers, 2011), 19.

[2] Timothy Demy, and Thomas Ice, Answers to Common Questions about the End Times, (Grand Rapids, Michigan: Kregel Publications, 2011), 89.

[3] Robert L. Thomas, Revelation 8-22: An Exegetical Commentary, (Chicago: Moody Publishers, 1995), 292-293.

Chapter 21

[1] James Oliver Buswell, A Systematic Theology of the Christian Religion, (Grand Rapids, Michigan: Zondervan Publishing House, 1973), 254.

[2] Tim LaHaye, and Ed Hindson, The Popular Bible Prophecy Commentary, (Eugene, Oregon: Harvest House Publishers, 2006), 443.

Chapter 22

[1] Francis Brown, S.R. Driver, and Charles A. Briggs, A Hebrew and English Lexicon of the Old Testament, (Oxford: Oxford University Press, 1978), 250-251.

[2] Robert L. Thomas, Revelation 8-22: An Exegetical Commentary, (Chicago: Moody Publishers, 1995), 270-271.

Chapter 23

[1] Henry Snyder Gehman, The New Westminster Dictionary of the Bible, (Philadelphia, PA: The Westminster Press, 1970), 620.

Chapter 24

List of Abbreviations

[1] Information taken from *The Chicago Manual of Style*, 16th ed., 2010, sections 10.45-51 pp. 510-514

LIST OF ABBREVIATIONS

Bible Name Abbreviations [1]

The Jewish Bible/Old Testament

Abbreviation:	**Book:**
Amos	Amos
1 Chron.	1 Chronicles
2 Chron.	2 Chronicles
Dan.	Daniel
Deut.	Deuteronomy
Eccles.	Ecclesiastes
Esther	Esther
Exod.	Exodus
Ezek.	Ezekiel
Ezra	Ezra
Gen.	Genesis
Hab.	Habakkuk
Hag.	Haggai
Hosea	Hosea
Isa.	Isaiah
Jer.	Jeremiah
Job	Job
Joel	Joel
Jon.	Jonah
Josh.	Joshua
Judg.	Judges
1 Kings	1 Kings
2 Kings	2 Kings

Lam.	Lamentations
Lev.	Leviticus

The Jewish Bible/Old Testament (continued)

Abbreviation:	Book:
Mal.	Malachi
Mic.	Micah
Nah.	Nahum
Neh.	Nehemiah
Num.	Numbers
Obad.	Obadiah
Prov.	Proverbs
Ps. (pl.Pss.)	Psalms
Ruth	Ruth
1 Sam.	1 Samuel
2 Sam.	2 Samuel
Song of Sol.	Song of Solomon (=Song of Songs)
Zech.	Zechariah
Zeph.	Zephaniah

The Apocrypha

Abbreviation:	Book:
Bar.	Baruch
Ecclus.	Ecclesiasticus (=Sirach)
1 Esd.	1 Esdras
2 Esd.	2 Esdras
Jth.	Judith
1 Macc.	1 Maccabees
2 Macc.	2 Maccabees
Pr. of Man.	Prayer of Manasses (=Manasseh)
Sir	Sirach (=Ecclesiasticus)
Song of Three Children	Song of the Three Holy Children
Sus.	Susanna
Tob.	Tobit

Ws	Wisdom (=Wisdom of Solomon)
Wisd. of Sol.	Wisdom of Solomon (=Wisdom)

The New Testament

Abbreviation:	Book:
Acts	Acts of the Apostles
Apoc.	Apocalypse (=Revelation)
Col.	Colossians
1 Cor.	1 Corinthians
2 Cor.	2 Corinthians
Eph.	Ephesians
Gal.	Galatians
Heb.	Hebrews
James	James
John	John (Gospel)
1 John	1 John (Epistle)
2 John	2 John (Epistle)
3 John	3 John (Epistle)
Jude	Jude
Luke	Luke
Mark	Mark
Matt.	Matthew
1 Pet.	1 Peter
2 Pet.	2 Peter
Philem.	Philemon
Phil.	Philippians
Rev.	Revelation (=Apocalypse)
Rom.	Romans
1 Thess.	1 Thessalonians
2 Thess.	2 Thessalonians
1 Tim.	1 Timothy
2 Tim.	2 Timothy
Titus	Titus

Versions and sections of the Bible

Abbreviation:	Book:
Apoc.	Apocrypha
ARV	American Revised Version
ASV	American Standard Version
AT	American Translation
AV	Authorized (King James) Version
CEV	Contemporary English Version
DV	Douay Version
ERV	English Revised Version
EV	English version(s)
HB	Hebrew Bible
JB	Jerusalem Bible
LXX	Septuagint
MT	Masoretic Text
NAB	New American Bible
NEB	New English Bible
NIV	New International Version
NJB	New Jerusalem Bible
NRSV	New Revised Standard Version
NT	New Testament
OT	Old Testament
RV	Revised Version
RSV	Revised Standard Version
Syr.	Syriac
Vulg.	Vulgate
WEB	World English Bible

[1] Information taken from *The Chicago Manual of Style*, 16th ed., 2010, sections 10.45-51 pp. 510-514

ABOUT THE AUTHOR

Fred Thompson is a Bible teacher and student of God's Word. He has taught classes and seminars on Bible prophecy. Thompson is an ordained minister credentialed for over 30 years with the Assemblies of God.

With a background in the worlds of engineering, business, and religion, Fred is able to apply his broad experience to understanding events in the world in the spotlight of scripture. He was called to ministry at mid-life and served twelve and one-half years on active-duty as a Navy Chaplain and an additional eight years as a Naval Reserve Chaplain. Dr. Thompson pastored Assemblies of God, Navy and Marine Corps congregations ashore and at sea.

A life-long learner, Thompson holds a Bachelor of Science in Electronic Engineering from Northrop University, a Master of Divinity from Fuller Theological Seminary, a Master of Arts in Human Development from Salve Regina University, and a Doctor of Ministry from Trinity Evangelical Divinity School.

He lives with his wife, Sandy in Meridian, Idaho.